ADDRESSES ON GOVERNMENT AND CITIZENSHIP

BY

ELIHU ROOT

COLLECTED AND EDITED BY

ROBERT BACON

AND

JAMES BROWN SCOTT

CAMBRIDGE
HARVARD UNIVERSITY PRESS
LONDON: HUMPHREY MILFORD
OXFORD UNIVERSITY PRESS
1916

COPYRIGHT, 1916
HARVARD UNIVERSITY PRESS

CONTENTS

	PAGE
INTRODUCTORY NOTE	vii
THE CITIZEN'S PART IN GOVERNMENT	1

Four Lectures delivered May 13, 14, 20, 21, 1907, at Yale University, under the William Earl Dodge Foundation.

EXPERIMENTS IN GOVERNMENT AND THE ESSENTIALS OF THE CONSTITUTION 77

The Stafford Little Lectures delivered at Princeton University, April 15 and 16, 1913.

NEW YORK STATE CONSTITUTIONAL CONVENTIONS OF 1894 AND 1915	119
TRIAL BY JURY, July 17, 1894	121
THE JUDICIARY, August 20, 1894	125
SECTARIAN EDUCATION, September 1, 1894.	137
THE POLITICAL USE OF MONEY, September 3, 1894 . . .	141
THE CIVIL SERVICE, September 21, 1894	145
THE PRINCIPLES AND PRACTICE OF CONSTITUTIONAL REVISION	147

An Address at a meeting of the Academy of Political Science, New York, November 19, 1914.

THE BUSINESS MEN AND THE CONSTITUTIONAL CONVENTION	155

An Address before the Merchants' Association of New York, March 25, 1915.

OPENING ADDRESS AT THE CONVENTION, April 6, 1915 . .	163
MAGNA CHARTA, June 15, 1915	169
IMPEACHMENT, August 20, 1915	173
ON ENDING THE SCANDAL OF THE LAW'S DELAYS, August 19, 1915	177
COURTS OF JUSTICE FOR SMALL CAUSES, August 23, 1915 .	185
THE REGULATION OF PUBLIC UTILITIES AND THE DECLINE OF THE "BLACK HORSE CAVALRY," August 25, 1915	187

iv   CONTENTS

"Invisible Government," August 30, 1915 191
Speech on Closing the Convention, September 10, 1915 207
A Study of the Proposed Constitution 213
    An Address at a dinner of the Republican Club of New York,
    October 18, 1915.
The New York Constitution and Representative
    Government 227
    An Address before the Economic Club of New York, October
    25, 1915.

GOVERNMENT 245
Acceptance of the New York Senatorship 247
    An Address to the Legislature of New York, January 28, 1909.
The Direct Election of United States Senators . . 257
    A Speech in the United States Senate, February 10, 1911.
Second Speech on the Direct Election of Senators . . 285
    A brief Address delivered in the United States Senate, May 23,
    1911.
The Case of Senator Lorimer 291
    An Address in the United States Senate, February 3, 1911.
The Banking and Currency Bill 323
    An Address in the United States Senate, December 13, 1913.
A Personal Statement 361
    Remarks in the United States Senate, December 16, 1913.
How to Preserve the Local Self-Government of the
    States 363
    A Speech at the dinner of the Pennsylvania Society in New
    York, December 12, 1906.
Address at the Conference of the Governors of the
    States 371
The Importance of Seeking Reform through State
    Governments 375
    Remarks at the tenth annual dinner of the National Civic
    Federation, New York, November 23, 1909.
The Spirit of Self-Government 379
    An Address at the one hundred and forty-fourth anniversary
    banquet of the Chamber of Commerce of the State of New
    York, November 21, 1912.

CONTENTS

THE ARIZONA CONSTITUTION AND THE RECALL OF JUDGES   387
A Speech in the United States Senate, August 7, 1911.

THE RECALL OF JUDGES 405
Remarks in the Republican State Convention at Rochester, April 10, 1912.

THE ADMINISTRATION OF JUSTICE 411

SOME DUTIES OF AMERICAN LAWYERS TO AMERICAN LAW .   413
Commencement Address before the Yale Law School, New Haven, June 27, 1904.

THE REFORM OF PROCEDURE 431
Presidential Address at the Annual Meeting of the New York State Bar Association, Syracuse, January 19, 1911.

JUDICIAL DECISIONS AND PUBLIC FEELING 445
Presidential Address at the Annual Meeting of the New York State Bar Association, New York, January 19, 1912.

THE INDEPENDENT BAR 463
An Address at the Dinner of the New York State Bar Association, New York, January 20, 1912.

REFORMS IN JUDICIAL PROCEDURE 467
A Statement before the Committee on the Judiciary of the House of Representatives, February 27, 1914.

THE LAYMAN'S CRITICISM OF THE LAWYER 479
An Address at the Annual Meeting of the American Bar Association, Washington, October 20, 1914.

THE SPIRIT WHICH MAKES A NATION LIVE 499
An Address at a Dinner of the American Bar Association, Washington, October 22, 1914.

THE LAWYER OF TODAY 503
An Address before the New York County Lawyers Association, New York, March 13, 1915.

INDIVIDUAL LIBERTY AND THE RESPONSIBILITY OF THE BAR   511
An Address at the Annual Dinner of the New York State Bar Association, January 15, 1916.

PUBLIC SERVICE BY THE BAR 519
Address as President of the American Bar Association at the Annual Meeting in Chicago, August 30, 1916.

INDEX 543

INTRODUCTORY NOTE

THE collected addresses and state papers of Elihu Root, of which this is one of several volumes, cover the period of his service as Secretary of War, as Secretary of State, and as Senator of the United States, during which time, to use his own expression, his only client was his country.

The many formal and occasional addresses and speeches, which will be found to be of a remarkably wide range, are followed by his state papers, such as the instructions to the American delegates to the Second Hague Peace Conference and other diplomatic notes and documents, prepared by him as Secretary of State in the performance of his duties as an executive officer of the United States. Although the official documents have been kept separate from the other papers, this plan has been slightly modified in the volume devoted to the military and colonial policy of the United States, which includes those portions of his official reports as Secretary of War throwing light upon his public addresses and his general military policy.

The addresses and speeches selected for publication are not arranged chronologically, but are classified in such a way that each volume contains addresses and speeches relating to a general subject and a common purpose. The addresses as president of the American Society of International Law show his treatment of international questions from the theoretical standpoint, and in the light of his experience as Secretary of War and as Secretary of State, unrestrained and uncontrolled by the limitations of official position, whereas his addresses on foreign affairs, delivered while Secretary of State or as United States Senator, discuss these questions under the reserve of official responsibility.

Mr. Root's addresses on government, citizenship, and legal procedure are a masterly exposition of the principles of the Constitution and of the government established by it; of the duty of the citizen to understand the Constitution and to conform his conduct to its requirements; and of the right of the people to reform or to amend the Constitution in order to make representative government more effective and responsive to their present and future needs. The addresses on law and its administration state how legal procedure should be modified and simplified in the interest of justice rather than in the supposed interest of the legal profession.

The addresses delivered during the trip to South America and Mexico in 1906, and in the United States after his return, with their message of good will, proclaim a new doctrine — the Root doctrine — of kindly consideration and of honorable obligation, and make clear the destiny common to the peoples of the Western World.

The addresses and the reports on military and colonial policy made by Mr. Root as Secretary of War explain the reorganization of the army after the Spanish-American War, the creation of the General Staff, and the establishment of the Army War College. They trace the origin of and give the reason for the policy of this country in Cuba, the Philippines, and Porto Rico, devised and inaugurated by him. It is not generally known that the so-called Platt Amendment, defining our relations to Cuba, was drafted by Mr. Root, and that the Organic Act of the Philippines was likewise the work of Mr. Root as Secretary of War.

The argument before The Hague Tribunal in the North Atlantic Fisheries Case is a rare if not the only instance of a statesman appearing as chief counsel in an international arbitration, which, as Secretary of State, he had prepared and submitted.

INTRODUCTORY NOTE

The political, educational, historical, and commemorative speeches and addresses should make known to future generations the literary, artistic, and emotional side of a statesman of our time, and the publication of these collected addresses and state papers will, it is believed, enable the American people better to understand the generation in which Mr. Root has been a commanding figure and better to appreciate during his lifetime the services which he has rendered to his country.

ROBERT BACON.
JAMES BROWN SCOTT.

APRIL 15, 1916.

THE CITIZEN'S PART IN GOVERNMENT

PREFATORY REMARKS

Gentlemen of Yale University:

In delivering the lectures of 1907 [1] on the responsibilities of citizenship, upon the foundation established by the late William Earl Dodge, I look back with pleasure to nearly forty years of friendship with Mr. Dodge, and to the example which his whole life gave of unselfish public spirit and of unremitting and intelligent effort for the welfare of his country and of his fellow-men. The establishment of this lectureship is but one of a multitude of acts which expressed his constant solicitude for the welfare of others and his grateful appreciation of all the blessings he owed to the just and equal laws, the liberty, and the opportunities of his country. His life was a better lesson in the responsibility of Christian citizenship than any lecturer can put into words; for he did what we write about and he proved what we assert.

It is my purpose to speak to you of your responsibilities regarding the government of your country and to discuss:

1. The task inherited or assumed by members of the governing body in a democracy.

2. The function of political parties as agencies of the governing body.

3. The duties of the citizen as a member of a political party.

4. The grounds for encouragement.

[1] These lectures were delivered at Yale University, May 13, 14, 20, and 21, 1907, under the William Earl Dodge Foundation, and were published and copyrighted by the Yale University Press in that year under the title "The Citizen's Part in Government." The editors acknowledge the courtesy of the Yale University Press in permitting their republication, and take this method of expressing their appreciation.

THE CITIZEN'S PART IN GOVERNMENT

I

THE TASK INHERITED OR ASSUMED BY MEMBERS OF THE GOVERNING BODY IN A DEMOCRACY

A LARGE part of mankind still regards government as something quite apart from the main business of life — something which is undoubtedly necessary to enable them to attend to their business, but only incidental or accessory to it. They plow and sow and harvest; they manufacture and buy and sell; they practice the professions and the arts; they write and preach; they work and they play, under a subconscious impression that government is something outside all this real business — a function to be performed by some one else with whom they have little or no concern, as the janitor of an apartment house, whom somebody or other has hired to keep out thieves and keep the furnace running. In reality, government is an essential part in every act of all this wide range of human activity. If it is bad, ruin comes to all; if it is good, success comes according to capacity and courage. The fairest and most fertile parts of the earth have been for centuries wilderness and desert because of bad government; not only lands capable of supporting multitudes in comfort and prosperity, but lands that have actually done so in the past, are today filled with wretchedness and squalor, with ignorance and vice, because of bad government; while under good government industry and comfort flourish on the most sterile soil and under the most rigorous climate.

The proportional part played by government in the personal affairs of every individual life is rapidly increasing. The crowding and complications, the inventions and improvements and coöperation of modern life have enormously increased the dependence of men upon each other. A century ago the farmers, who made up the bulk of the people of the United States, were quite independent in their comparatively isolated lives and with their few wants. I can recall a picture drawn by one who remembered the life of that time upon a farm familiar to my childhood. He said:

> We had abundance of food and clothing; we raised our own wheat and corn, which were ground into flour and meal at a neighboring mill for a share of the grain; we raised all the beef and pork and vegetables that we required; we raised sheep and sheared them, and carded and spun and wove the cloth for our winter clothing; we raised flax and from it made our own linen; we dipped our own candles, which afforded sufficient artificial light for a life in which it was the rule to rise with daylight and go to bed when it was dark; we had milk from our own cows, eggs from our own fowls and abundant firewood from our own forest. We had everything we needed except money and we had little need for that; the chief occasion for its use was to pay the small taxes which were required each year. There was little money in the community and it was sometimes hard to get enough to meet the taxes.

Under such conditions, government might well have been regarded as an outside affair, of which the less people heard the better.

Compare such a life with that of a resident in one of the cities, in which a third of the population of the United States are now crowded together. The city family is dependent for every article of food and clothing upon the products of far-distant places. These products are supplied through great and complicated agencies of transportation, and for the most part have been prepared for use by a variety of distant mills and factories. The family depends upon fuel brought from distant coal mines; its light comes from gas and electrical plants over which it has no control; the habits of business and social life are all adjusted to means of communication furnished by great telegraph and telephone companies and a government postal service. It exercises no control at all over the things that are absolutely necessary to its daily life. A strike in the coal mines, like that which occurred in Pennsylvania five years ago, may at any time put out not only the furnace but the kitchen fire; a strike in the lighting plants, like that which happened in Paris a few weeks ago, may plunge the house and the neighborhood into darkness. A quarrel between railroad companies and their employees, or the inability of a railroad company to furnish sufficient transportation, may cut off the most necessary supplies; the meat is liable to be diseased unless some one inspects the packing-house, the name and place of which no one in the family knows. The milk may be full of tuberculosis and the water full of typhoid germs unless some one has tested the cattle and some one enforced sanitary ordinances upon distant farms. Access to the house depends upon a street department, safety from thieves upon a police force, and freedom from pestilence upon the sanitary disposal of the sewage of thousands of other families. Under these circumstances of complete interdependence, the individual is entirely helpless. The only way in which he can compel the continuance of conditions under which he and his family can go on living is by combination with others equally dependent with himself, and by organization for whatever control over those conditions is necessary. That combination and organization is government.

Men may leave all this part of the business of life to others and treat it as no concern of theirs; men may voluntarily elect to play no part in the control of the affairs which make up their daily life and to play no part in the working out of the great questions upon which the prosperity of their country, the future of their children, and the welfare of the race depend; but they need not flatter themselves that these things are matters apart from them, or that they are leading free and independent lives. Abstention is impossible under the conditions of modern life and modern popular government. Men must either govern or be governed; they must take part in the control of their own lives, or they must lead subject lives, helplessly dependent in the little things and great things of life upon the will and power of others.

The theory and practice of government have vastly changed within the past few centuries and especially within the last century and a half. Control by superior authority, claiming by divine right, selected by inheritance, and supported by a comparatively small governing class selected in the same way was repressive and directive. Government was then apart from the main and general activities of life, but it was apart from them by being above them, by exercising rights over them and making them all pay tribute. Under our modern systems of popular government the repressive function still continues, but entirely new and different modes of action have been developed. The repression is self-repression, and the direction is the resultant of internal forces determining the character of the directed mass. Popular government is organized self-control — organized capacity for the development of the race. It is the good and noble impulses and the selfish and cruel passions of man struggling with each other for the maintenance or the denial of justice; it is the lust for power and savage instinct for oppression struggling against manhood and self-respect for the maintenance or destruction of liberty; it is the greed and cunning that have shamed the history of the world struggling with honesty and virtue for public purity; it is the longing in the heart of man for better things up through education to broader knowledge and higher life; it is the vast elemental forces of humanity moving great masses of men in violent protest against the ills of life, to the destruction of social order; it is the instinct of self-preservation which rallies other multitudes in defense of vested interests and traditional rights; it is the dreams of Utopia to be realized by changing everything and the reverence for the past that is horrified by changing anything. These tremendous forces express themselves in laws, in the enforcement of laws, in contempt for laws, in good administration and bad administration, in sudden outbursts of feeling altering the surface of things, and in gradual movements affecting the whole relation of nations toward the ideals of peace and order and justice and righteousness. Upon them and the results they work out depend the prosperity, and honor and life of nations, and the future of civilization; and upon them depends the value of every farm and factory and shop, of every bond and share of stock, the peaceful prosperity of every home, the opportunities for success of every child.

Heavy responsibilities were assumed and serious dangers were confronted in departing from the theory that government must come from above, that the selfishness and cruelty and lust of mankind can be successfully controlled only by a class of superior men, by a small number of specially qualified experts in the art of government bred to power and trained in its exercise; and in adopting the idea that the great masses of men, who had always been subject to repression, control, and direction, could be trusted to govern themselves without any superior control; that by a process of evolution, through education and practice, the popular mass would acquire the self-restraint, the soberness of judgment, the loyalty to the fundamental principles of justice and liberty necessary to stable and effective government. The new departure was regarded by many of the wisest and best of mankind with the most gloomy forebodings. There was widespread belief that when political power was vested in the poor they would promptly proceed to divide among themselves the property of the rich, and that the control of democracy would prove to be the tyranny of the mob — the most frightful form of oppression mankind has yet known. Jack Cade and Wat Tyler rebellions, peasant insurrections, the Red Terror of the French Revolution, the excesses of the Commune of Paris, the reign of assassination in Russia, the Jacquerie in Roumania, the perpetual revolutions of undeveloped Latin-America, have seemed to give color to these anticipations.

We have been accustomed to flatter ourselves that the great American experiment has been successful. It has indeed carried the demonstration of popular capacity of the people to rule themselves far beyond the point which originally seemed possible to the enemies of popular government. That demonstration has produced an effect upon the constitution of government throughout the civilized world by the side of which the Roman dominion sinks to an inferior place as a permanent force. Under its influence the whole continent of South America took heart and gathered courage to throw off the hard colonial yoke which held its people under the subjection of the Iberian Peninsula, and, passing through the storms of internal strife and continual revolution, is gradually emerging into a condition of peaceful industrialism. Its influence reacted upon France and requited her assistance in the cause of our independence, by furnishing proof of the possibilities of humanity to her political philosophers. It inspired the hope that led to the tempestuous revolt against the French Monarchy, which, through many vicissitudes, has resulted in the French Republic, now for more than a third of a century stable in its peaceful sway. Its example reacted upon England in the series of reforms which began with the Reform Bill of 1832 and enabled that conservative people to impress upon their ancient monarchy the essentials of a real government by the people, in which justice and liberty are preserved in a very high degree.

The fact that for more than a century peaceful industry, respect for law, and individual freedom have been maintained under popular government in the United States, and that they have been accompanied by extraordinary material prosperity, has fostered a tendency toward popular government in every country of Europe.

Nevertheless, we must not delude ourselves with the idea that the American experiment in government is ended or that our task is accomplished. Our political system has proved successful under simple conditions. It still remains to be seen how it will stand the strain of the vast complication of life upon which we are now entering.

Notwithstanding the change in the source of power, which has been the fundamental fact in the development of popular government, that government has proceeded hitherto with much respect for inherited governmental traditions and methods. The old machinery for the application of governmental power to the life of the community has been in a great measure preserved. Legislative bodies have made laws, and courts have sat in judgment under them and executives have enforced them, under authority derived from the people, very much as they did under authority derived from a superior power, except that the spirit has been different and the responsibility has been different. It remains to be seen whether democracies will be willing to continue these methods of government, or whether, with their continually increasing realization of their own power, they will change the old methods of government along such lines as are foreshadowed by the proposals for the initiative and the referendum — proposals that would substitute direct democratic action for representative government, as representative government was substituted for absolute monarchical control; and it remains to be seen what the effect of that kind of government would be.

Notwithstanding the great change at the top involved in the setting aside of monarchical and aristocratic government in modern republics, the substance of the old social system, with its respect for the rights of private property, has been preserved. Modern democracy has simply engrafted upon that system an assertion of the right of equal individual opportunity, so that no barrier of birth or caste or privilege shall stand between any man and whatever career his ability and industry and courage entitle him to achieve. The very basis of that social system is now widely questioned. Socialists, in no negligible numbers, demand a reorganization of society upon entirely different principles; limitations upon the right of private property are widely favored; and limitations upon individual opportunity are still more widely enforced among all that part of the wage-workers who believe in putting a limit upon the amount of work which each workman shall be permitted to do in his day's labor, so that the most industrious, skillful, and ambitious workman shall be permitted to do no more and to earn no more than the most dull, idle, and indifferent workman. A common benefit of property and a common standard of exertion are liable to be substituted for all inequalities of fortune and achievement. After many centuries of struggle for the right of equality there is some reason to think that mankind is now entering upon a struggle for the right of inequality. It remains to be seen how democracy will work under these new conditions.

One thing we have learned during the experience of popular government is that the progress of the world has carried civilized people to a point where we are not now voluntarily trying the experiment of government by self-control, but where society must rely upon that and cannot possibly go back to the old method of keeping peace by force or the threat of force. The complication and interdependence of life puts the power of doing incalculable harm in the hands of so many men and combinations of men in different occupations that a realization of common interest is absolutely essential to the working of the vast machine. The mere forcible enforcement of law is quite inadequate. It is not fear of the policeman or the sheriff that keeps the peace in our many cities; it is the self-control of the millions of inhabitants enabling them to conform their lives to the rules of conduct necessary to the common interest; it is only against the exceptional lawbreaker, and criminals who are comparatively few in number, that the policeman and sheriff are effective.

Another thing we have learned is that it is possible for men to set up abstract and impersonal standards of right conduct, such as the great rules of right embodied in our constitutions, and that, although each man in his own personal affairs tends to depart from the standard and struggle against its application to himself, the general agreement of all who do not at the time happen to have any adverse interest is competent to maintain the standard in force and effect; so that all men may give their adherence and support to standards of conduct ethically superior to the course which the vast majority of them desire to take in their own affairs.

Another lesson the experience of popular government has already made plain is that the art of self-government does not come to men by nature. It has to be learned; facility in it has to be acquired by practice. The process is long and laborious; for it is not merely a matter of intellectual appreciation, but chiefly of development of character. At the base of all popular government lies individual self-control; and that requires both intelligence, so that the true relation of things may be perceived, and also the moral qualities which make possible patience, kindly consideration for others, a willingness to do justice, a sense of honorable obligation, and capacity for loyalty to certain ideals. Men must be willing to sacrifice something of their own apparent individual interests for the larger interests of city, state, country; and without that willingness successful popular government is impossible. This loyalty to an abstract conception is a matter of growth. It is easy to trace its development in our own country from the time when local allegiance was predominant to the time when national allegiance has become predominant. Intense devotion to the state is one of the great elements of strength in the Japanese nation now; it was one of the chief elements in the growth of Roman power. It cannot be produced except by a long-continued habit of effort and sacrifice in a common interest. It is this gradually acquired loyalty to country more than anything else that enables men to exercise the self-control necessary to the subordination of the narrower personal interests to broader general interests, upon which self-government depends. The individual selfishness which fills men with a controlling desire for personal aggrandizement, to the exclusion of any consideration for the general good, marks a low stage in the political development of every country that has a history; and the bitterness of internal dissension which leads the adherents of particular opinions or interests to insist upon them at the cost of ruin and death to adherents of opposing views in the same country must in its turn give way to the conception of the higher loyalty before there can be really successful popular government. There must be both the habit of self-control and the dominating influence of the common ideal to enable men so to act together, subordinating minor differences of interest and opinion, as to make popular government possible.

The countries in which the people are continually engaged in internal quarrels never progress. History is full of such examples. Some races appear to be incapable of combining in the support of a common political ideal beyond a certain point. The races that have this capacity to the highest degree persist and rule the world; the peoples that have it to a low degree lose their national entity and cease to govern. There are many countries now where controversy regarding matters of inferior importance is a present bar to progress. In every living nation the question always remains, How far has it capacity to go in that kind of combined action which subordinates individual interests, the interests of groups and localities and classes, to the general good of the country? That limit must be found in the capacity for development of the individual characters that make up the nation.

The Greeks appeared to be unable to maintain any effective combination beyond the individual city; the idea of a Hellenic country acquired no control over their lives. When the supreme moments were passed in which they united to repel the Persian invasions, they immediately fell apart and resumed their quarreling with each other. The Peloponnesian and Delian Confederacies, which might as well have been the foundations of a common country as the confederation of the American colonies, served merely as opportunities for the selfish advantage of Sparta and of Athens. So Greece, with all its glories of art and literature and oratory, went down before nations of inferior intellectual capacity — first the Macedonians and then the Romans. The long period during which internal strife has prevailed in the Latin-American countries has been an illustration of the struggle between the capacity for self-control in a common national interest and the forces of selfish individualism and factionalism. The major part of those countries are now happily emerging from the stage of militarism and the condition of continual revolution into the stage of industrialism and stable government; but in some of them on the borders of the Caribbean the struggle is still waged and the result is in doubt. The discord between the thirteen American states and the practical paralysis of the Continental Government before the Constitution of 1787 illustrates the failure to attain this necessary condition; and the union of the same states under the Constitution illustrates success. The downfall of the once powerful Kingdom of Poland illustrates the triumph of those discordant motives which make successful government impossible. United Italy and Germany; the stability which the French Republic has maintained for a third of a century after so long a period of tumult and discord; the unbroken bonds that unite Great Britain with her colonies; and the permanence of the American Union, mark the great advances of which civilized men generally have proved themselves capable, in applying the principles of combination for a common national interest. No one can tell, however, when or where the great new forces which are being developed in the course of government by the people, and especially in the relations between industrial and social changes and the political constitution of government, will overcome the power of common and patriotic purpose that makes possible combined national action

Our country is not safe in leaving unused any possible influence and effort toward the maintenance and growth of patriotic idealism and practical loyalty.

There are probably few readers of history who do not ask themselves the question whether the civilization of our time is to pass through its cycle of development and decay, yield to the disintegrating passions of human nature, and leave the world to begin the process again as it has so often done. Is the New Zealander indeed to stand on the ruins of London Bridge? The question that Macaulay asks still remains to be answered:

Is it possible that in the bosom of civilization itself may be engendered the malady which shall destroy it ? Is it possible that institutions may be established which, without the help of earthquake, of famine, of pestilence, or of the foreign sword, may undo the work of so many ages of wisdom and glory, and gradually sweep away taste, literature, science, commerce, manufactures, everything but the rude arts necessary to the support of animal life ? Is it possible that, in two or three hundred years, a few lean and half-naked fishermen may divide with owls and foxes the ruins of the greatest European cities — may wash their nets amidst the relics of her gigantic docks, and build their huts out of the capitals of her stately cathedrals ? [1]

Is some future poet to sing of us that " the lion and the lizard keep the courts where Jamshýd gloried and drank deep " ? If not, I think the difference must be found in the fact that popular government carries our civilization down to the foundations of society and spreads it so widely over the surface of the earth. Former civilizations were but islands surrounded by vast regions where savagery ruled; and they were but civilizations at the top, underlaid by the ignorance and prejudice of a multitude who had no interest in preserving what such civilization had gained, no capacity to appreciate its merits, and but little contribution to make toward its increase. They were the civilizations of privileged classes, which always tend toward degeneration. The hope for the permanence of modern civilization is that it is being built up from the bottom through the participation of the whole people in that universal, combined action for the common good which we call popular government.

It may seem that I have ascribed a part to government which properly belongs to the development of morals and the spread of education; but I think a little reflection will show that this is not so. Morals do not develop in the abstract, but in the gradual adaptation of conduct to rules already intellectually accepted. The conduct to be adapted is conduct toward other real living beings. Even in the

[1] Mill's *Essay on Government*. Macaulay in *Edinburgh Review*, 1829.

purely personal relations government plays a leading part in directing conduct, as in the changing rules of law regarding the rights and duties of owner and slave, master and servant, employer and laborer, parent and child, guardian and ward; but in the great field of the relations of men to each other in the mass the whole development of morals practically is governmental. The words liberty, justice, order, peace, protection of the weak, public purity, public spirit, denote the application of certain moral ideas to the conduct of men in mass toward their fellow-men. The tremendous power of a people become sovereign and the helpless dependence of modern men upon each other make this phase of development of morals of primary and vital importance. It is the conversion of moral rules into political conduct that concerns government, and that is a process of practical experimental life working out results acceptable to a majority and then enforced by them upon the minority. This process is not much furthered by mere insistence upon the rules, or by academic discussion of them, for in successive generations the same accepted moral rules are translated into entirely different conduct, and it is the translation which is of vital importance.

If we turn to education, we find that instead of this being a thing apart, the education which enables the great body of democracy to work out the problems I have described — the primary education, which opens the door of knowledge to the mass and the door of unlimited opportunity to the exceptional intelligence — is almost universally supplied by government as a part of the political qualification for citizenship. On the other hand, it is very doubtful whether the higher academic education contributes much to capacity for political usefulness. As a rule, political wisdom, in the best sense, comes in life and not in study, and the tendency of highly educated men to neglect all political duties is unfortunately too general. It is the process of government that educates for government. It is experience and observation of the working of laws and political practices and injurious customs that point the way to intelligent legislation. The factory inspectors in the state of New York inspected over thirty-eight thousand separate factories last year. Those inspections and the reports and the discussions on them are education through which the thirty-eight thousand employers and the million and odd employees and the community which controls them both, may come to a sense of just how the balance ought to be held between the employer's rights of property and free contract, on one hand, and the employee's freedom from the slavery of circumstance, and the state's right to have normal, healthy citizens, on the other.

The greatest, most useful educational process ever known in the world occurs every four years in the United States when, during a presidential election, some fifteen million voters are engaged for months in reading and hearing about great and difficult questions of government, in studying them, in considering, and discussing, and forming matured opinions about them. We sometimes hear complaints that elections interfere with business and come too frequently. On the contrary, nothing else is so valuable and important for business, because it is this educational process that is laying the solid foundation of sound judgment, sober self-restraint, and familiarity with political questions among the governing mass, upon which the security of all business depends.

Doubtless there have been abuses in raising and applying campaign funds; but, in the main, there is no more useful expenditure of money from the public point of view than this, which in the last presidential election, according to official statements, amounted to only about three and a half cents per capita for the people of the United States, on one side, and probably somewhat less on the other; for the great bulk of it is applied to the political education of voters.

Everything that I have said about the relations of government to our modern life — the character of popular government, its difficulties, its dangers, its possibilities, its mode of life and growth — carries, as a necessary corollary, the existence of a universal duty of citizenship to take part in it. It is not rightly a matter of choice whether a man shall trouble himself about affairs of government in his community, or confine himself to his business, his profession, or his pleasures, and leave others to govern; it is a matter of peremptory obligation which cannot be avoided by any intelligent man who has any understanding of the conditions under which he lives. A French nobleman could attend the court of Louis XIV, or retire to his castle, as he chose, without discredit; for under that system of government the question was whether certain men or certain other men conducted the government. The essential feature of the present condition is that the burden and duty of government rest upon all men, and no man can retire to his business or his pleasures and ignore his right to share in government without shirking a duty. The experiment of popular government cannot be successful unless the citizens of a country generally take part in the government. There is no man free from the responsibility; that responsibility is exactly proportioned to each man's capacity — to his education, to his experience in life, to his disinterestedness, to his capacity for leadership — in brief, to his equipment for effective action in the great struggle that is continually going on to determine the preponderance of good and bad forces in government, and upon the issue of which depend results so momentous to himself, his family, his children, his country, and mankind. The selfish men who have special interests to subserve are going to take part; the bitter and malevolent and prejudiced men whose hearts are filled with hatred are going to take part; the corrupt men who want to make something out of government are going to take part; the demagogues who wish to attain place and power through pandering to the prejudices of their fellows are going to take part. The forces of unselfishness, of self-control, of justice, of public spirit, public honesty, love of country, are set over against them; and those forces need every possible contribution of personality and power among men, or they will go down in the irrepressible conflict. The scheme of popular government upon which so much depends cannot be worked successfully unless the great body of such men as are now in this room do their share; and no one of us can fail to do his share without forfeiting something of his title to self-respect.

II

THE FUNCTION OF POLITICAL PARTIES AS AGENCIES OF THE GOVERNING BODY

WE have now reached a point where the question is naturally suggested: How should the citizen take part in the government of his country? Given a young American who has just completed his academic training and is about to begin his active life, and who wishes to do his full duty as a citizen in maintaining and improving his government: where is he to begin and what is he to do?

On the threshold of the answer to this question we must determine that the duty will not be fulfilled merely by playing the rôle of a critical observer of what others do. It is indeed important that there should be criticism; no public officer can afford to be relieved from it. Every man in the performance of public duty tends to lose his sense of proportion by seeing things from only one point of view, and tends to devote himself unduly to some phases of his work, which preoccupy his mind, so that he neglects other things which ought to have his attention. Every one makes mistakes, and the sooner he is told of them the better; and every one who is obliged to withstand the pressure which conflicting interests bring to bear upon the performance of his duty finds in the certainty of criticism a powerful incentive to be sure that his action is such that he can defend it afterwards according to his own convictions of right. Criticism tests and corrects the opinions and the practices of the men who are doing the work of the world.

Nevertheless, to criticise is not to do the work. The preservation and development of civilization require affirmative forces; the real work of life is constructive; criticism is destructive.

It is, moreover, true that the most valuable criticism comes from the men who are also undertaking to do things themselves. Criticism always involves comparison with some standard assumed in the critic's mind; and the value of the criticism depends largely on the conformity of that standard to the real conditions under which the work criticised is done. The critic of government who is himself trying to do his share of the affirmative work of government is in the way of learning something of the evils against which other men engaged in government are struggling, the difficulties they have to overcome, the means they have at their command with which to overcome those difficulties, and the real as distinguished from the apparent value of what they do. Criticism from such a source is a real benefit. The mere critic of government, however, who does not himself attend to his share in the affirmative work of government, ordinarily adopts standards of comparison which ignore the most important elements of truth, and he is quite likely to do more harm than good; he gradually assumes an attitude purely destructive and acquires a habit of simple fault-finding. Such a man is generally a hindrance rather than a help to the work of good government.

It is equally plain that for most men preaching to others about what they ought to do is not a very effective way of helping along the work of government. Mankind does not pay much attention to people who talk down at them from without about their duties, unless the instruction comes from some one who is already recognized by his own performance as having acquired the right to be considered a teacher. Occasionally a man has some message to deliver of such weight and cogency as to impress itself upon many other minds; but such men are very rare and very far removed from the ordinary run of men. If any one can express as much wisdom as President Eliot has put into some of his addresses, or can write such a book as President Hadley's *Freedom and Responsibility*, or such a book as James Bryce's *American Commonwealth*, or John Morley's *Life of Gladstone*, or can compose such orations as Edmund Burke's, he can make a real contribution to the science, and therefore to the practice, of government. But for the generality of us whose knowledge and insight are not much, if any, superior to those of the great body of our fellows, it is wise to wait until we have at least greater experience than they have in the things we undertake to talk about, before we try to play the schoolmaster to them.

There are many people whose idea of duty is to assign duties to others, but for the most part their efforts are a mere waste of words. Mr. Murat Halstead once told me how, being a young newspaper correspondent during the Civil War, he had felt moved to write a long letter to Secretary Stanton, giving his view about the matters in which the Secretary was engaged, and how, many years afterwards, this letter was found on the files of the War Department indorsed, in Stanton's own handwriting, " M. Halstead — Tells how the war ought to be carried on." At the time of our conversation, a long and ripe experience had taught the veteran journalist the true character of his youthful undertaking; and he remarked that this indorsement was the only evidence he had ever known that Stanton possessed real humor. The world is full of men ready to tell how the war ought to be carried on by others; but the war goes on just the same, and the men who bear the burden and heat of the struggle in actual service accomplish the results, and their self-constituted and little-qualified advisers have really no substantial part in the business.

It is plain that the true way to begin an active part in the affairs of government is not by being elected or appointed to office; that should always be a result rather than a beginning of interest, activity, experience, and proved capacity in the affairs of government. This is especially true of the greater offices. As to the smaller offices, especially those which occupy the entire time of the officer, it is often very undesirable for a young man of education and good parts to abandon his profession or business or whatever calling he would naturally follow to fill one of them. There are very few public offices in comparison with the number of citizens, and at the best only a very small part of the young men of the country could enter into active governmental work by holding them.

Of course, voting is a fundamental and essential part of the qualified citizen's duty to the government of his country. The man who does not think it worth while to exercise his right to vote for public officers, and on such public questions as are submitted to the voters, is strangely ignorant of the real basis of all the prosperity that he has or hopes for, and of the real duty which rests upon him as a matter of elementary morals; while the man who will not take the trouble to vote is a poor-spirited fellow, willing to live on the labors of others and to shirk the honorable obligation to do his share in return.

Merely voting, however, is a very small part of the political activity necessary to popular government. An election is only the final step of a long process by which the character of government is determined. The election records the result of the process; the real work of government is in the process.

The voter ordinarily has merely a choice between two or three candidates for an office, no one of whom may be the man whom he would prefer for the office; or he has the opportunity to say yes or no to some question framed in advance, and very likely framed in such a way that neither yes nor no would represent his real opinion upon the subject or lead to what he would regard as a satisfactory result. Of course our election laws preserve the theoretical right of each voter to cast his vote for any one whom he chooses; but we all know that if the voter exercises that right for some one other than a foreordained candidate his ballot goes into the category of scattering votes and is practically thrown away. The same thing which is true as to the limitation of the voter to particular candidates is true also of the issues or opinions those candidates are supposed to represent. The issues are all made up before the voter goes to the polls. You and I may feel a desire to express an opinion by our ballots on the revision of the tariff, or on free trade and protection, or on the regulation of railroads, or on the prevention of trusts, or on the method of taxation, or on economy and honesty of administration, or on the currency and banking system, or on the control of insurance companies, or on the powers of corporations, or on the open shop, or on the foreign policy of the country; but when we go to the polls merely as voters we are entirely helpless as to determining upon what question our votes will count, and ordinarily as to which way they will count upon many of the questions in which we are interested. The questions on one side or the other of which our votes will weigh, have all been selected and brought into prominence long before the election. The result of this is to limit the effect of our votes to certain narrow channels. The issues as finally framed may not be those we think most important, and the relation of the candidates to them may be such that we cannot help one cause by our vote without hurting another in which we are equally interested. The men who are elected to office give practical effect when in office to the results of that previous process recorded in the canvass of votes. Thus, the chief work of popular government is to be found in the process which results in the vote.

Under our present political system in the United States and at our present stage of political development, that process is mainly carried on through the organizations known as political parties.

Manifestly, there must be organization; there must be some means by which the vast number of questions which arise in relation to government in our complicated modern life shall be simplified; by which the questions that are vital shall be separated from the comparatively unimportant questions and the people who tend to think alike upon the vital questions may have an opportunity to make their votes effective by voting alike; by which, from the vast number of men who are available for selection to administer the powers of government, some may be indicated as the probable choice of a sufficient number of voters to give some chance of success in voting for them.

If you can imagine all the sixteen hundred thousand voters of the state of New York, for example, going to the polls on an election day with no previous concert of action, but each determined to vote for the best man — that is, each determined to vote for the man who of all his acquaintance seems to him the best to fill the position, or for the man whose opinion most closely agrees with his upon some subject which happens to be uppermost in his mind — what would be the result! what thousands of names would be found upon the ballots when they came to be counted! If a majority of voters were required to elect, of course there would never be an election. If only a plurality of votes were necessary to elect, the largest number of votes cast for any one man would inevitably be a very small proportion of the total of votes cast. It is highly probable that the great majority of the voters would have preferred that the man with the plurality should not be elected, and would have been quite ready to agree on some one else whom they all preferred to him and considered but little less desirable than the various persons for whom they had cast their scattering ballots. The men elected in such a way would have no guide as to the principles, or policies, or rules of conduct which the majority of the voters wished them to follow in the offices to which they were elected.

Such a method of conducting popular government, however, is not merely futile, it is impossible; for human nature is such that long before such an election could be reached some men who wished for the offices would have taken steps to secure in advance the support of voters; some men who had business or property interests which they desired to have protected or promoted through the operation of government would have taken steps to secure support for candidates in their interest; and some men who were anxious to advance principles or policies that they considered to be for the good of the commonwealth, would have taken steps to secure support for candidates representing those principles and policies. All of these would have got their friends and supporters to help them, and in each group a temporary organization would have grown up for effective work in securing support. Under these circumstances, when the votes came to be cast, the candidates of some of these extempore organizations would inevitably have a plurality of votes, and the great mass of voters who did not follow any organized leadership would find that their ballots were practically thrown away by reason of being scattered about among a great number of candidates instead of being concentrated so as to be effective.

Under very simple social conditions, especially in the smaller governmental subdivisions such as towns and counties, and in some parts of the country where there are important questions involved in the local government and almost every one in the community is well known, so that elections are largely a matter of personal choice, this kind of purely personal organization and effort often answers the purpose of enabling voters to concentrate their ballots effectively. Several well-known men may offer themselves publicly as candidates and each of them carry on, through a personal organization, a campaign for the suffrages of his fellow-citizens. In the governmental affairs of the country at large, however, and for the most part in the governmental affairs of the states, the opportunity for personal choice is very limited; it is impossible that any man should be really personally known to a very large proportion of the people in the United States, or even in any state. There are questions of government upon one side or the other of which the voters hold strong opinions; and men are known and are commended to the voters as candidates by the positions they have taken upon those questions, and, if they have already held office, by public report of the way in which they have performed their duties in carrying out certain policies or applying certain rules of conduct. Candidates, therefore, in these larger fields are regarded chiefly as the representatives of principles and policies, and so far as they are affected by personal popularity, that is chiefly based upon the effectiveness with which they have already represented those principles and policies.

These great governmental questions are not temporary and special to particular elections. There are some questions of policy which are never settled permanently, because new conditions are always arising to serve as occasions for their reconsideration. For example, the subject of a protective tariff has furnished questions upon which the people of the United States have divided for a century, and probably will divide for an indefinite time to come. These tariff questions reappear in one form or another at every national election when they do not happen to be for the moment thrust aside by some other special and absorbing issue. The fact that the people have decided in favor of a high tariff at one time, or for a low tariff at another time, has no effect whatever to prevent the same old battle being fought over and over again.

Series of questions relating to the extension of slavery, merging into the questions relating to the continuance of the war for the Union, and these merging again into the questions relating to the results of the war and the political and economic status of former slaves, have continued from the beginning of the nineteenth century to the beginning of the twentieth. In the same way a long dividing line may be seen separating people of different ways of thinking upon questions relating to the currency. In one form or another, for a long series of years, the controversy has been waged between the advocates of currency based upon a gold value, on the one hand, and the advocates of a currency based upon the idea that the Government can give it value in the form of greenbacks or depreciated silver, on the other.

There are certain distinct and fundamentally opposed schools of thought and opinion which range portions of the people on different sides of many questions through long series of years. For example, the people of the United States during most of our national existence have been divided between the advocates of a strict construction and the advocates of a liberal construction of the Constitution. One would confine the powers of the National Government within the narrowest possible limits; the other would find in the Constitution all the powers that any nation can have except as they are expressly limited by the terms of the Constitution. One tends to carry the independence of local self-government to an extreme; the other tends to carry the centralization of national government to an extreme. This fundamental difference of view has divided the people of the country in a long series of successive elections upon many specific and important questions; upon the power of the National Government to carry on internal improvements; to restrict the extension of slavery; to establish a national bank; to charter Pacific railroads; to maintain a tariff for protection as distinguished from a tariff for revenue only; to acquire and incorporate in the United States additional territory; to acquire and govern so-called colonial possessions; upon the extent of the power to regulate commerce, of the taxing power, of the police power, of the treaty-making power.

It is true that in recent years some professed disciples of Jefferson have advocated measures of national control which would have led that apostle of the least government possible to regard Hamilton as a strict constructionist; but these are probably temporary aberrations. The same division between the two schools of interpretation of the Constitution still exists and in the nature of things must continue.

With these continuing questions and permanently divided schools of opinion the association of the advocates of each opposing view is bound to be repeated in many successive political campaigns. This association is not occasional and fortuitous; it is, to a great extent, predetermined and customary. The men who entertain positive views upon one side or the other of the great political questions become known; they acquire the habit of working together; they rely upon each other's coöperation. The association is practically continuous, because the process in which the advocates of these differing views are engaged is continuous. Our people are so constituted that no sooner is an election over and the result declared than the supporters of the defeated candidates and the advocates of the rejected views immediately begin their efforts to secure a reversal of the result at the next election. The ever-present consciousness that in a year, or two years, or four years there will be an opportunity to substitute victory for defeat is a great element in the peaceable and good-natured acceptance of the results of our elections by those who are defeated. The very intensity of the minority's belief that its candidates and its policies are better than those which for the time being have a majority of the votes creates an expectation that when the test of performance is applied to the successful candidates and the test of application is applied to the accepted policies, their inferiority will be demonstrated, so that the public verdict will be reversed.

This continuous association and effort on the part of a great number of men for the accomplishment of a common purpose through a continuous series of political struggles of course involves continuous organization, for the work of a great number of men for a common purpose through a long period of time cannot be carried on at all without organization. These continuous, voluntary, organized associations to secure the adoption of policies upon which their members agree and the choice of officers who will represent those policies are what we call political parties.

As new issues arise under the changing needs and difficulties and desires which time brings to every community, they find these organizations already in existence, and if the new issues are such as to demand settlement or excite great interest among the voters it becomes immediately necessary for the existing political organizations to determine what positions they will assume upon the new questions. This determination is naturally based either upon the application of the general principles of government and the general ideas of policy which have controlled the respective parties, or upon an estimate of the support which one position or another will receive from the voters of the country, or upon a combination of the two. Sometimes the lines which separate the voters of the country upon one side or the other of a new question run across lines of cleavage between the old parties, and the comparative importance of the new question is such that great bodies of voters dissolve their association with an old party and form a new association with another party; as, for example, the positions taken by the Democratic and Republican parties on the subject of the currency a few years ago led many gold Democrats to go over to the Republican party and many free-silver Republicans to go over to the Democratic party. Occasionally, the attitude of all existing parties is so unsatisfactory to the people much interested in a new question that they undertake to form a new party for the furtherance of their views on that particular question. Generally, these attempts show that the people who are interested by a particular new issue over-estimate its importance and their attempts to form a new party fail; but we have had one signal example the other way — in the formation of the Republican party in 1856 by the men who were not satisfied with the attitude of either the Democratic or the Whig party in regard to the extension of slavery. As a rule, however, each old political party adds to the list of principles and policies which it advocates a view upon each great new question in accordance with the opinions of a majority of its members, and, with some slight changes and realignment of dissatisfied members, old parties go on representing their membership upon the new questions as well as upon the old questions in reference to which their parties were organized. In time, as the original questions which led to the formation of a party disappear, the party continues with an organization representing its members no longer for the specific purposes which brought them together, but for the new purposes which they have agreed upon through the processes of their party organization and activity.

Many very good and public-spirited men have deplored the existence of parties, and some of them prefer to stand altogether aloof from political parties and to exercise their right to express their opinions by voice or pen or print, and to vote with entire personal independence and without being either trammeled or helped by the coöperation of others.

As I have tried to point out, however, political parties are the natural product of evolution in the process of popular government; they are not merely the best and most practical way in which the operations of popular government can be carried on, but they furnish the only way to carry on those operations so far as we can judge from the experience of the world up to this time. In no large country has any real popular government ever existed for any considerable time without them. They exist in England, France, Germany, Austria-Hungary, Italy, in all the constitutional governments of Europe, and in the Latin-American states, with variations depending upon the characters of the different peoples; and in every case they assume more definite form and more clearly recognized functions as the country progresses from the status of personal government to government of principle and policy. As popular government develops, in every case political parties develop, and in every case the longer the operations of popular government have continued and the more perfect is the expression of public opinion and will, the more highly developed in the true sense is political party organization.

It is, of course, highly important that the voters of a country should hold themselves at liberty to condemn by their votes any party with whose policy they do not agree, or which is false to its professions, or whose candidates for office are found to be unfit to represent truly the principles professed; nevertheless, the great mass of the people of the United States at every election go with one of the great parties or the other, and the great mass of the voters of each party stay with their party election after election. They approach every election with a presumption in favor of the policies advocated by the party to which they have adhered in the past. As to the majority of them, that presumption is never overcome. Their minds are most receptive to arguments and persuasion coming from their own party associates and in favor of their own predilections. The habit of reliance upon party leaders; instinctive loyalty to old comrades in former political struggles; the natural reluctance to break old associations and form new ones; and often the predisposing effect of inherited opinions and youthful training — all combine to make men vote ordinarily with their party. This settled tendency makes the determinations reached in the councils of the great political parties the most important and dominating factors in determining the course of popular government, and renders participation in party action the most effective way to reach the mind and influence the action of the mass of voters. The great work of popular government is done in the associations and primaries and caucuses and conventions, in the conferences and discussions and canvassing and personal association, in the private meetings and public meetings, in the convention committees, in the drafting of platforms, in the struggles between candidates for nomination, in the efforts to educate and convince and persuade voters, and in all the great and complicated process which goes on incessantly within each party in every village and town and city and state, culminating in the submission of the work of the national convention to the voters of the country at large, and, upon one side or the other, determining the legislative and executive policies of the country.

I have no doubt that the American who feels the responsibilities of his citizenship can do his duty as a part of the governing people better by entering into the organization of one of the great political parties than in any other way. The better educated, more intelligent and more active he is, the greater is the reason why he should seek for his powers the immense increase of effectiveness which comes from association, combination, and organization. There are many abuses of party power and in party management in the United States; but the American who stands apart and criticises or condemns the conduct of political parties may well be answered, "Yours was the responsibility and you have wholly failed to discharge it."

We sometimes hear it said by intelligent and educated men that there is no opportunity for them to do anything in party politics because the machine controls everything, and no one who is not in the machine has any chance — that is to say, that the men who for the time being hold the party offices will control the party action, and the voice of an individual new recruit in the party ranks would not exercise any control. This is wholly fallacious. There never is a party organization or a so-called machine which cannot at any time be turned out of power if the rank and file of the party choose to turn them out; and there never is a time when a man of character and ability entering into the active work of a party cannot gain in full measure the influence and power to which his ability entitles him, or cannot contribute materially to a change of control, provided he is willing to take the pains and give the time and effort necessary to the creation and exercise of influence among the members of the party. Of course a new recruit cannot step into a new association with a great number of people and immediately dictate what they are to do. Time and long-continued effort and long association, through which come confidence in a man's sincerity and respect for a man's opinions and a desire to comply with a man's wishes, are necessary to the exercise of that kind of power; but the same things are necessary to the exercise of influence and power in any of the affairs of life which involve the conduct of others. If any American citizen is willing to make the same sacrifice of personal comfort and convenience and employ the same ordinary means to make himself an active force in politics which he would employ to make himself an active force in business, or in the church, or among the members of any profession, or in any kind of enterprise which involves the action of a large number of men, no party machine can prevent and ordinarily no party machine wishes to prevent him.

We often hear remarks made which indicate an impression that politicians are rather a low set of fellows, with selfish aims and corrupt practices, who manipulate party politics for their own advantage, and that the less self-respecting gentlemen have to do with them the better. If that is ever the case, and it undoubtedly is the case at some times and in some places, it is always because at such times and in such places political control is allowed to go by default. Such a condition of political affairs is always due to the fact that the citizens who are honest, upright, and public-spirited, who would not prostitute party power to personal advantage, who would not make a party organization a corrupt combination to secure place and profit, fail in the performance of their public duty and permit the party organization which limits and restrains the exercise of their political powers to remain in the hands of unworthy and self-seeking men. There is no party in which the great body of the voters desire that kind of control, and it cannot exist unless the voters of the party, and the citizens who ought to be active in exercising the powers of the party, fail through indifference and unwillingness to spend the necessary time and take the necessary trouble to exercise the powers that lie within their reach. I have said that there are serious evils incident to the management of our political parties, and some of these I shall presently mention; but they are all evils which would be readily remedied if the citizens generally who are in agreement upon the principles of the respective parties would recognize their responsibility and perform the political duties which rest upon them as citizens. The fact that such evils exist, instead of being a reason for not engaging in party activity, is a reason for engaging in it. Such a fact presents a clear and imperative duty to remedy the evil; and that duty rests not merely upon the men who already have membership in the party, but upon all men who agree in general with the principles of the party, and who therefore ought to look upon the party officials and managers as their agents and to hold themselves responsible for their agents' character and conduct.

Another reason or excuse for not taking part in political affairs is the direct reverse of those that I have mentioned: it is that party management is satisfactory; that matters go along very well, and that a man does his duty to his party if he supports its ticket with his vote and perhaps contributes his fair share toward the payment of its expenses. This position can never be maintained. It means, in the first place, that the man who takes it is willing to have the greater part of his duty as a self-governing citizen done for him by others, and it means also that the power and efficiency of the party in working out the problems of government and in advocating and enforcing the conclusions which it reaches are reduced by the desertion of one of its elements of power — that is to say, the ability and force of character of a part of the men who ought to be engaged in its work.

None of these reasons for not taking part in party politics is ordinarily the real reason. The real reason is that men are unwilling to spend the time and the money and the labor necessary for the due performance of their duties as citizens; that they prefer to attend to their professions, their business,

THE CITIZEN'S PART IN GOVERNMENT 37

their pleasures, and allow others to govern them rather than to take part in governing themselves; that they are willing to permit the great struggle which is continually proceeding for the preservation and protection of their property, their liberty, their opportunities, for sound principles of finance, for the preservation of society, for the correction of social and political and business evils, for the punishment of wrongdoing, for the furtherance of justice and the maintenance of peace and righteousness, to go on without any help from them. They are willing to let the great mass of men upon whose education and clear and reasonable understanding of governmental questions the whole structure of free government depends go without any help from their education and intelligence. They are willing to pursue a course which, if shared in by the rest of their countrymen, would bring our constitutional government to an immediate end, wreck our prosperity, and stop our progress. They are willing to depend, for the continuance of everything they have of value in life, upon their confidence that others will be more public-spirited and unselfish and willing to take trouble in performing their public duties as citizens than they are themselves.

III

THE DUTIES OF THE CITIZEN AS A MEMBER OF A POLITICAL PARTY

It is quite simple and easy for any intelligent young man to take part in the activities of a political party in the United States. He has only to select the party the ascendancy of which he considers most desirable, and let the recognized party officials of his own home know that he is willing to work. He will promptly find himself admitted to membership in whatever may be the simplest form of political organization or association in the locality, and will find himself provided with plenty of work to do. He cannot begin by leadership or by dictating party policies, and he probably cannot assume in the beginning any such position of superiority as he may think his education and intelligence entitle him to have. The work in which he will be engaged at first may be simply the details of local organizations, which will perhaps seem of little consequence; or engaging in struggles between candidates for small offices, in which he does not take very much interest; or canvassing from house to house to ascertain the political affiliations or preference of the residents. It may be very far from that advocacy of principles and influence upon the policies and direction of government in which he would like to engage. He may, however, be sure that he will ultimately find the exact level and rise to the full height of opportunity and influence and dignity of employment to which his abilities, character, and devotion to his duties entitle him. If he is able and willing to render effective service, he will gradually find himself moving along until he is at last engaged in the most important duties on the broadest fields of political action. In the meantime, or if he should never rise above mere local activity, let him remember that the first and chief duty of citizenship is to serve in the ranks — not to await some great and glorious occasion to win fame and power. It is the active service of the men in the ranks that makes the difference between popular self-government and popular submission to an absolute monarch. Without the great body of workers who never rise to leadership popular government would be as impossible as a successful army composed entirely of officers.

In the performance of the simple duties of the political beginner there are certain principles of conduct so indispensable to usefulness that observance of them is a clear duty.

Men influence the conduct of others chiefly through personal association and intercourse. There is such a preponderance of good in human nature that association with men ordinarily begets a liking for them. As men come to know each other each comes to receive from the others the respect and confidence to which he is entitled; his character and his opinions insensibly acquire their due weight and influence. It is not the stranger who says, "Go there," or "Do that," who is obeyed; but it is the old acquaintance who says, "Come with me," or "Let us do thus and so," who is followed. The knowledge of the tendencies and prejudices of men acquired through personal acquaintance makes the suggestion of a wish from a friend often of greater weight than the most eloquent speech or the most profound essay from a stranger. This power of association is the chief thing which enables political organizations, even when they are going wrong or in bad hands, to resist attacks from without, even from best and most highly respected citizens, when these occasionally and for the moment are moved to instruct the men actually engaged in political affairs as to what they should and should not do.

There is no monopoly of this power of association. Unselfish and public-spirited men can qualify themselves to exercise it if they take the trouble, just as well as self-seeking men of low aims.

To accomplish very much with other men one must have a considerable degree of sympathy with their feelings and interests. The man who never cares or thinks about anything but himself cannot expect anybody to think or care about him. If he has no interest in the hopes and ambitions of others, no consideration for their sensibilities, they will be equally indifferent so far as he is concerned. Political bodies, especially primary political bodies, are made up, to a degree unequaled in any other association, of men of widely varying conditions in life, with different opportunities for knowledge and capacity for reflection, with different prejudices and ways of thinking, differing widely in information, in previous reflection, in breadth and scope of thought, in motives, in characters, in tempers, in ambitions. Each one of them is entitled equally with all the others to have his opinions, his wishes, and his ambitions considered; and the feeling that any one gives kindly consideration to them is in itself a great source of influence. The man who has never had anything above a day's wages or a small clerk's salary, or who perhaps has no income but is looking for one, is just as much entitled to aspire to a place in the custom-house, or to a post office, or to be a letter-carrier, as the very successful and able man distinguished in his community, is entitled to aspire to be governor or senator; and the small man is just as much entitled as the big man is to have his aspiration considered and treated as an honorable aspiration. The small trader who hopes that the legislation and administration of government will be such as to promote the prosperity of his little business is just as much within his rights as the great banker who hopes for currency legislation or the great manufacturer who hopes for tariff legislation beneficial to his business. Sympathetic recognition of such considerations is a natural and necessary basis for influence and leadership among political associates.

A rightly constituted man brought into association with a great number of others cannot fail to acquire some degree of proper humility. It matters not how well educated or intelligent a man may be, the combined experience, knowledge of life, range of thought, fertility of suggestion, thoroughness of criticism, to be found in any great body of men taken together are so far beyond him that he is bound gradually to take an attitude of receiving and learning as well as endeavoring to instruct and lead. He will thus escape from the fatal attitude which ruins one's influence with others by giving an impression of assumed superiority in wisdom or virtue.

In order to secure united and successful action for any purpose the members of a political party must learn to subordinate minor differences in order to combine for the advocacy and promotion of more important matters in which they agree. That is essential to the maintenance of any political organization, as indeed it is essential to successful combination in all human affairs. The concerted action of many men of different interests, impulses, opinions, and desires is essential to the accomplishment of any result under popular government; and that concerted action cannot be attained except by continual and mutual compromises. There is no quality in a people more important for success in popular self-government than that practical common sense which makes them capable of such practical compromises; and every one engaged in political affairs is under a duty to make such fair concessions from his opinions and desires as may reasonably contribute toward bringing out practical and effective results in common action. Of course this does not mean to compromise character. Every man, however, should be careful not to deceive himself into supposing that to be a matter of conscience which is really only a matter of pride of opinion, or determination to have one's own way.

In politics, as in everything else, a man ought to be thinking about his work and not about what he is going to get out of it; to be intent on succeeding in his undertakings rather than upon the appearance that he is making or the credit that he is going to receive. That is an essential condition to success in all the arts which deal with human nature as their material. I have often noticed at the bar that the advocate who is thinking about making a fine speech never makes a lodgment in the mind of either the court or the jury; they may admire the speech, but they are neither convinced nor persuaded. This is true at the bar, in the pulpit, and in the lecture room. It is equally true of literary style; all obtrusively fine writing is ineffective. And this is true in politics. I do not mean to insist upon an impracticable altruism, or to exclude an honorable ambition to succeed and to have the reward of good, effective work, which comes from the favorable opinion of one's fellows and a general recognition of one's service. Recognition and appreciation are properly gratifying to every one; but that should be a secondary object if a man is to do the best type of work. The primary object with every man should be to do the work that comes to his hands just as well and thoroughly as he possibly can do it; and there is one certain reward for work so done — in the satisfaction that the man himself feels in having done good work. Every man should rely for the appreciation and recognition of his service, not upon his own estimate of it, but upon the estimate of others; no man can properly judge of his own merit or the value of his service. It will often happen that particular things a man does may not receive from others the credit to which they are entitled; but it will also happen that he will get more credit than he is entitled to for other things that he does; and, in the long run, every man may be sure that he will receive all the credit to which he is entitled without any attempt on his part to influence the judgment of others or to force upon them his own estimate of himself. The man who engages in political work with the primary idea of getting office may succeed in getting the office; but he is likely to lose what is of far greater value than any office — the good opinion of the community in which he lives — for the people of self-governing communities ordinarily possess a strangely unerring insight which detects the spirit in which such a man works and classifies him as a mere politician in the bad sense of the term and stigmatizes him as an office-seeker.

The career and influence of such a man, moreover, tend to promote the kind of political activity which is the most injurious and demoralizing in popular government.

It appears from what I have already said that there are three quite distinct stages in the development of self-government. The first and lowest is that in which the people of a country divide with sole reference to their partisanship for particular persons whom they desire to put into power. In its worst form this kind of partisanship is so completely exclusive of consideration for public good that the contest for personal ascendancy often merges into violence and civil war and continuous revolutionary attempts. This condition was once widely characteristic of Latin-American republics, and some of them are still at that low stage of development, although many of them and the most important have happily passed out of that stage and have come to regard the choosing of officers as the means of giving effect to policies rather than as being itself the object of popular government. Those countries have had one preëminently great and noble example.

José de San Martin was born in Argentina, served with distinction under the Spanish flag in the Napoleonic wars, and returned to his native land at a critical period of the

South American struggle for independence. Everywhere except in the United Provinces of the River Plate the early revolutionary efforts had been suppressed by Spain. The old vice-royalty of Peru, strong in its mountains, in its army, and its command of the sea, was the center of reactionary power. Impregnable there against attack, it seemed that Spain could choose her own time to sweep down over the old trade route by which the precious metals of Peru had found their way to the commerce of the Plate and to destroy all that was left of South American freedom. San Martin conceived the great design of leading an Argentine army across the Andes, conquering the Spaniards in Chile, setting that country free, creating a navy on the Chilean coast, destroying Spanish naval power in the Pacific, and, having acquired command of that ocean, attacking and overcoming the Spaniards in Peru along the same line of approach from the west that had been followed by the old *conquistadores*. He executed his design with amazing audacity, tenacity of purpose, power over men, organizing skill, and self-devotion. He overcame obstacles apparently insuperable, achieved one of the really great military and political movements of history, and ruled in Lima as " Founder of the Liberty of Peru." In the meantime, Bolivar had led successful revolution in Venezuela and Colombia, and the union of the northern and southern patriot forces seemed about to complete the eradication of Spanish rule in the Southern Continent.

The character and conduct of Bolivar soon made it plain that he regarded San Martin as a rival, that they could not coöperate, and that the continuance of both commands meant strife for personal power between the two leaders — to the destruction of the patriot cause. Then San Martin gave an example of self-sacrifice more admirable than his victories or his strategy. In order that a united patriot army might oppose the forces of Spain, he effaced himself, laid down his command, his titles, his dignities, and power. He sent to Bolivar his pistols and his war horse with this note:

Receive, General, this remembrance from the first of your admirers, with the expression of my sincere desire that you may have the glory of finishing the war for the independence of South America.

And he left the scene of his great achievements never to return. Bartolomé Mitre says truly:

History records not in her pages an act of self-abnegation executed with more conscientiousness and with greater modesty.

San Martin died misunderstood and in exile. To the generals and politicians who were plunging the South American republics into continual bloodshed for their own selfish ambitions, and to their adherents, the spirit of self-assertion which demands power and fame seemed admirable and the spirit of self-effacement for a cause seemed weakness. But as the people of those countries have risen to a higher plane of duty and honor, there has come the realization that the great South American — the one worthy to be named with Washington as the example and inspiration of patriotism — was the modest soldier who cared more for his cause than for his office, and who was willing not merely to wield power, but to give up power, for his country's good.

It has always seemed to me that Mr. Tilden pursued a very patriotic and commendable course when the election to the presidency was in question between him and Mr. Hayes in 1876. The election was very close and there was no doubt that if all the votes actually cast in the Southern States received effect Mr. Tilden would be declared elected; but many votes had been thrown out by the state returning boards in the South on account of alleged fraud and intimidation that had prevented the casting of other votes, which, if cast, would probably have caused a different result. There was a question that inevitably would have resulted in civil war in any country where the personal idea was predominant in politics, and there were in this country many men of high character and standing who urged that Mr. Tilden's title to the office should be asserted by armed force; but he was decided and immovable in the position that he would permit no breach of the peace of the country in his behalf, whether he got the presidency or not. The questions were finally submitted to a special court devised for the purpose, and that court by a majority of one decided in favor of Mr. Hayes. So Mr. Tilden lost the presidency; but he gained what was of far greater value — a title to the esteem and gratitude of all good citizens. He probably rendered a greater and more permanent public service than by anything he could have done as President.

The second stage of development in popular government is reached when the people of a country have passed beyond exclusive attachment to individual fortunes and, turning their attention to questions of principle or policy or material interest, have arrayed themselves in support of their various opinions or desires, but have not yet reached the point where they are able to subordinate minor considerations upon which they differ to those of primary and vital importance upon which they agree. In this stage of development many groups make their appearance, each having some controlling idea which it regards as of primary importance. Sometimes those ideas are local; sometimes they are religious; sometimes they relate to special class or business interests; sometimes they relate exclusively to some special political, social, or economic question. The most conspicuous result of such a condition is found in the election of legislative bodies, in which representatives of all the different groups are found, and in which no party has a majority; so that no affirmative legislation is possible except by trades and combinations between different groups. One effect of this legislative condition is that in countries where the executive is responsible to the legislature the executive cannot depend upon steady and constant support from the law-making body in any line of policy, because the combination of groups is continually changing and the executive that has a majority today may find itself in the minority tomorrow. There are some countries where this government by groups exists, in which the constant fluctuation of legislative combinations and majorities leads to very frequent changes in the responsible ministry; and in those countries good administration is almost impossible, not only because there can be no continuity of executive policy, but because the heads of the executive departments who constitute the ministry are seldom able to do more than to begin to learn their business before they are turned out to make place for new men, who have again on their own account to begin the same process of learning the business. The most corrupt and unsatisfactory period in the government of Great Britain was when Parliament was divided into groups in this way.

Great Britain has passed out of that stage into the third and higher stage of development, in which two great political parties oppose each other upon fundamental differences, the members of each differing in many respects among themselves upon minor questions but not allowing those differences to break up their party. This condition now exists both in England and in the United States. Under it the executive government has the continuous support of its own party, and so long as that party is in the majority there is a united and effective government. When that party ceases to command the support of a majority of the people, it goes out of power and the other party comes into power to receive an equally effective support until another change comes.

The course of evolution in popular government is thus from the formation of an indefinite number of individuals into parties with the idea of putting men into office, to the formation of an indefinite number of parties grouped especially with regard to advancing special interests and ideas, and thence to the formation of two great parties representing fundamental differences in the general principles and policies of government. The development is from the unmixed preponderance of personal and selfish motives to the predominating motive of common good for the country.

Since personal selfishness and desire for personal aggrandizement are by no means eradicated from human nature, there is a constant tendency in political parties to revert to a lower type. Party leaders frequently use for their own personal advantage the power conferred upon them for advocacy of those ideas which the members of the party believe to be for the best interests of the country. This tendency is promoted by every man who takes part in political activity with the primary purpose of getting an office for himself, and it is discouraged and reduced by every man who takes part in political affairs with the primary purpose of doing effective service to advocate the principles that he believes in and to elect officers who will apply those principles, leaving the question of his own personal reward and advantage to come from such recognition of his service as others may think it deserves.

The tendency to revert to the lower type of organization which concerns itself solely in the obtaining of office is one of the evils to which I referred in a former lecture when discussing the objections sometimes urged against taking part in politics. This evil has been very prevalent in American politics, and it is still prevalent, although to a less extent than formerly. With us it takes the form of grafting upon the great parties of voters organized for the advocacy of certain declared principles an organization of active party workers for the distribution of offices.

The process is a very plain and natural one. The object for which the voters have associated in a party is to bring about the application of certain principles and conformity to certain policies in carrying on the government of the country. The only way to secure that is by agreeing upon and voting for candidates for office who, if elected, will observe those principles and follow those policies. There is an immense number of these offices, of varying grades, from the presidency down; there are national and state, county and city, town and village officers, legislative and executive and judicial officers; great numbers of clerks and collectors, inspectors and watchmen, agents of different kinds, mechanics, and skilled and unskilled laborers. Comparatively few of these, and generally the most important, are actually elected by the people; the great mass of them, particularly of the minor officers and employees, are selected and appointed by the officers who have already been chosen by election, and about this selection and appointment the people have nothing to say except as individuals among them may make requests or recommendations to the appointing powers.

The proper and necessary operations of a party cover a wide field of activity. They include the selection of candidates for the elective offices. This is done sometimes by means of the direct expression of the wish of the voters of the party, but more frequently by having the voters of the party elect delegates to conventions which meet and select the candidates. The operations of the party also include the consideration, discussion, determination, and statement of the position of the party upon the important public questions of the day. This also is done by the same conventions which select the candidates. The operations of the party also include appeals to the people to vote for the candidates which represent the party. These appeals are made by personal canvasses from house to house, by public meetings and speeches, by the circulation of campaign literature through the mails and through the columns of the press. There are also included the general and concerted efforts to get out the vote, to see that the voters of the party do not, through indifference, stay at home and neglect to vote at all; and also the manning of the polls under concerted and systematic arrangement, for seeing that the voters of the party are not denied their rights at the polls, and that no fraud is perpetrated or undue advantage is taken by the members of the other party in the voting or the counting of the vote. All these things require an immense amount of hard work and the participation of a great number of men, and all these workers have to be directed. System, organization, control, leadership, are absolutely necessary; leadership of opinion in the framing of platforms and in the selection of proper candidates, and leadership of administration in the carrying on of the work.

This enormous mass of work preceding and leading up to the exercise of the franchise and, so far as we can judge both from reasoning and experience, essential to make the ballot effective, is done by volunteers, who receive no compensation from the state for the public service they are rendering and must be inspired by some other motive. So well established is the understanding that these are the processes by which Americans work out the results to be confirmed by the ballot, that laws have been made in the larger states, where political affairs are most complicated, to regulate proceedings in the political parties by primary laws designed to prevent fraud in the selection of delegates to conventions and in the choice of candidates.

It is not at all unnatural that among the men who do this voluntary work resulting in the selection of candidates and their election to public office there should be many who desire to be appointed to the offices and employments at the disposition of the officers so elected. Unfortunately, there has grown up in the United States a practice of considering the service of party workers leading to the selection and election of candidates as a controlling reason for the appointment of those party workers to the places at the disposal of the candidates after their election; and that practice has resulted in the prevalent understanding that there is an implied agreement by every successful candidate for an elective office to reward support by exercising his governmental powers for the appointment and employment of his supporters. The practice originated in the complicated political activities of the great states of New York and Pennsylvania early in the last century. It was extended to the Federal Government under the presidency of Andrew Jackson, and the most familiar statement of it was made by William L. Marcy in the Senate of the United States in the debate on Jackson's nomination of Martin Van Buren to be minister to England. Marcy said:

> It may be, sir, that the politicians of New York are not so fastidious as some gentlemen are as to disclosing the principles on which they act. They boldly preach what they practice. When they are contending for victory, they avow their intention of enjoying the fruits of it. If they are defeated, they expect to retire from office; if they are successful, they claim, as a matter of right, the advantages of success. They see nothing wrong in the rule that to the victor belong the spoils of the enemy.

The application of this principle is not confined to the demand of the individual party worker upon the successful candidate for a recognition of his personal service; it goes a step further back and affects the action of the party worker in the selection of party leaders who will support and press the party worker's claim to recognition from the public officer when elected. It determines the selection of the party committees and their chairmen, from the lowest local committee in the assembly district or town or village, who are expected to press the claims of the men who elect them for appointment and employment, up through the county and state committees to the national committee and the chairman of the national committee, who directs the vast machinery of the presidential election. It converts the whole party organization commissioned by the voters of a party to conduct the systematic proceedings which shall enable them to maintain and advance their political principles by their votes, into an organization primarily for the parceling out of offices, and incidentally for the promotion of party principles so far as may be necessary to keep the voters of the party from repudiating the party organization.

Several results follow from the application of this principle.

It leads to a selection of candidates for office based primarily on their supposed willingness to carry out the implied obligation to use their official powers, if elected, for the reward of their party supporters, the fitness of the candidates and the benefit which the public will receive from their service being considered only when it is probable that an election will be close and that every vote will be needed.

It leads to the exercise of the appointing power by the public officers who are elected in this way, not with reference to the public service which the appointees can render, but with reference to the political service which they have already rendered in the selection and election of the officer. It goes farther than this in its effect upon the exercise of official power, for by natural extension it is made to cover an assumed obligation on the part of public officers in the performance of their other duties to act, not with reference to the public good, or for the promotion of the great policies of a party, but in such a way as to secure the greatest number of offices with the greatest possible emolument to the members of the party organization. This obligation is assumed to rest upon legislators, and sometimes even upon judges.

It demoralizes the public service, by establishing a tenure of office which depends not upon faithful and efficient service to the country, but upon service in party primaries and caucuses and conventions; and it tends to make the elected officers feel responsible not so much to the public opinion, which judges of their fidelity and efficiency, as to the party managers who are to determine whether they shall be renominated or not. This cannot fail to result in poor service. It is impossible to have good service in any business, public or private, unless the character of the service itself is to determine whether it shall continue. This has been very well illustrated in a way which any one who has been in the habit of frequenting the city of New York during the past twenty years can appreciate. That city formerly had a street-cleaning department managed by a bi-partisan police board composed of two Democrats and two Republicans. The members of the street-cleaning force were appointed for the political committees of the two parties. The party committees and the party leaders in the different assembly districts in the city were furnished with tickets, which they distributed to their supporters. On the presentation of these tickets the holders were treated as entitled to employment on the force. Their retention on the force depended entirely on the favor of the party managers from whom they got their tickets — not at all upon the way in which they did their work. They were lazy, inefficient, undisciplined, and without effective supervision, because under that system no supervision could have any effect; and the streets of New York were continuously disgracefully filthy. The evil became so great that the legislature at Albany changed the law and provided for a superintendent of street cleaning; and about that time one of the occasional revolts of the city of New York occurring, a good business man was made mayor and he appointed Colonel George E. Waring, of Newport, a distinguished sanitary engineer, superintendent of street cleaning. Colonel Waring threw overboard the whole existing system, established a rigid system of supervision, paid no attention to so-called political claims, and promptly dismissed every man who was found to be lazy or inefficient. Within a few months he had an active and effective force; the streets of the city were swept clean and kept clean, and they continued so until Colonel Waring's lamented death and for a long time after, until the system which he had inaugurated gradually fell into disuse and the old habit of using the street-cleaning department as an opportunity for giving employment on the grounds of party service was resumed; and the city has become again disgracefully unclean.

The application of the principle announced by Senator Marcy tends to weld the official personnel of party organization into a compact body of men, who, depending upon each other for personal advancement, stand by each other at all hazards and oppose the power of organization to every effort on the part of the mere voting members of the party to take any course in party action which may interfere with the regular business of bartering offices for support and support for offices. As the men who form such a compact official organization expect to make their living by it, they are able to devote their entire time to the manipulation of party affairs, and in that way have a great advantage over the business and professional men, who must devote themselves to their business and professions and can give but a small part of their time to political activity.

Another and peculiar result of this system is the creation, in some places where the system is in full force, of double governments, one carried on by the executive and legislative and judicial officers provided for by law, the other carried on by the official organization of the party which happens to be in the majority, under the direction of the party leader, who controls the action of the lawful officers. There have been cities in which substantially the whole board of aldermen have invariably and without question voted as they were directed by the leader of the majority party in the city, and upon all important questions have waited habitually to get his orders before voting; in which the executive and administrative officers have sought his instructions rather than the instructions of the mayor, and in which the minor judicial officers have uniformly conformed their judgments to his wish. There have been states in which the party leader has habitually determined what bills should and what bills should not be passed by the legislature, and in which the majority of the legislature have uniformly sought and obeyed his instructions. The lawful officers are thus subservient to the party leader, because they hold their offices at his will by virtue of the compact organization behind him, which will control future conventions, nominations, elections, and appointments.

A peculiarity of this kind of government is that the real governing power is without legal responsibility and is practically free from statutory legal restrictions. The party leader combines legislative and executive functions, and he often trenches upon judicial functions. He acknowledges no obligations to the public; his obligations are simply to secure offices for his followers. To pay a legislator for his vote, or an executive officer for the exercise of his discretion, is a felony, and for an officer to receive a bribe is a felony; but the party leader is under no legal prohibition against receiving any consideration or acting upon any personal interest in the exercise of his power, which controls both the vote of the legislator and the discretion of the executive. The only danger he has to apprehend is that the voters of his party may repudiate his candidates, and against that he is measurably protected by the fact that such action will be at the cost of putting the government into the hands of those who would administer it upon principles and according to policies which the voters consider unsound and injurious.

Such a system is not essential to effective party organization. On the contrary, it tends to prevent effective party organization; it tends to keep out of the organization the men whose service would be most effective, and to make more difficult the work of the men who take part in the organization with the real purpose of making it accomplish its legitimate results. It tends to make an organization which does not really represent the voters of the party, and to leave the voters of the party without any genuine representative organization. It results in elections in which the voters of the country have no opportunity to express by their ballots their real choice of candidates or their real opinions upon public questions. It weakens one of the great agencies for carrying on a popular government and introduces an injurious imperfection into the method by which alone public opinion can be made effective through governmental machinery.

The whole system is pernicious and discreditable to American citizenship. It ought to be done away with and political parties ought to be brought back to the sole performance of their proper function as organizations for the promotion of principles and policies, free from the control of mere office-trading combinations.

It is, however, mere folly to say that the existence of such an evil furnishes a reason why educated, self-respecting Americans should not take part in the work of the political parties with which they vote. On the contrary, the existence of the evil presents a manifest and urgent duty to the conscience and patriotism of every competent American.

The duty is to enter into the work of party activity and help make the party organization what it ought to be. The

THE CITIZEN'S PART IN GOVERNMENT 57

duty rests upon each intelligent citizen in his own community to incite the voters of the party he believes in to take charge of their own affairs, and to substitute party organization and party leadership which are really representative of them in place of the party organization and the party leadership which are maintained by the distribution of office for the sake of office.

If one is to judge the world and the conduct of men by comparison with a standard of ideal perfection, of course everything will be found wrong. If the question we ask is whether the world, or any community in it, is good or bad, right or wrong, we must recognize a painful degree of error and selfishness, and injustice and cruelty, and indifference, and ignorance.

The true question, however, is not what the world is, but what its tendencies are. Is it moving towards better things, or worse? Is the level rising, or falling? Mark the condition and character of civilized peoples in successive centuries or generations, and see whether liberty and justice and righteousness have been gaining, or losing. See whether education has gained ground, or lost; whether men generally are more, or less intelligent; whether they have grown more cruel, or more kindhearted; more selfish, or more regardful for the rights of others; whether government is more pure, or more corrupt; whether the laws are more, or are less just — more, or less respected. Thus you will learn whether to look to the future with confidence and hope, or with distrust and with forebodings.

You will find that such an inquiry yields a most cheerful and encouraging response as to the condition and probabilities of popular government.

There is not one element of character, of capacity, or of practice going to make up what government ought to be in which there has not been steady and great advance in the progressive development of government by the people.

It is impossible to read an account of the life of the people of any civilized country in any past century without finding an amazing degree of cruelty, of oppression, of immorality, of corruption, and of class privilege regardless of common right, which has now been substantially done away with.

THE CITIZEN'S PART IN GOVERNMENT

To go no farther back than the early years of the last century in England, the reform of the criminal law, under which more than two hundred offenses were punished by death; the struggle for Catholic emancipation; and the revolution in parliamentary representation, which destroyed the rotten borough system and transferred power from the landed aristocracy to the great middle class in England, mark the positions from which popular government has advanced.

If we go back to the early days of the eighteenth century John Morley says:

A candid and particular examination of the political history of that time, so far as the circumstances are known to us, leads to the conclusion that Walpole was the least unscrupulous of the men of that time.

Yet he says:

... That Walpole practiced what would now be regarded as parliamentary corruption is undeniable. But political conduct must be judged in the light of political history. Not very many years before Walpole a man was expected to pay some thousands of pounds for being made Secretary of State, just as down to our own time he paid for being made colonel of a regiment. Many years after Walpole, Lord North used to job the loans, and it was not until the younger Pitt set a loftier example that any minister saw the least harm in keeping a portion of a public loan in his own hands for distribution among his private friends. For a Minister to buy the vote of a Member of Parliament was not then thought much more shameful than almost down to our own time it has been thought shameful for a Member of Parliament to buy the vote of an elector.[1]

Lecky says of Walpole and his times:

He governed by means of an assembly which was saturated with corruption, and he fully acquiesced in its conditions and resisted every attempt to improve it. He appears to have cordially accepted the maxim that government must be carried on by corruption or by force, and he deliberately made the former the basis of his rule. ... The systematic corruption of Members of Parliament is said to have begun under Charles II, in whose reign it was practiced to the largest extent. It was continued under his successor, and the number of scandals rather increased than diminished after the Revolution. Sir J. Trevor — a Speaker of the

[1] *Walpole*, By John Morley. London. 1889. In *Twelve English Statesmen* Series.

House of Commons — had been voted guilty of a high crime and misdemeanor for receiving a bribe of 1,000 guineas from the city of London. A Secretary of the Treasury — Mr. Guy — had been sent to the Tower for taking a bribe to induce him to pay the arrears due a regiment. Lord Ranelagh, a paymaster of the forces, had been expelled for defalcations in his office. In order to facilitate the passing of the South Sea Bill, it was proved that large amounts of fictitious stock had been created, distributed among, and accepted by, Ministers of the Crown. Aislabie, the Chancellor of the Exchequer, was expelled, sent to the Tower, and fined. The younger Craggs, who was Secretary of State, probably only escaped by a timely death. His father, the Postmaster-General, avoided inquiry by suicide, and grave suspicion rested upon Charles Stanhope, the Secretary of the Treasury, and upon Sunderland, the Prime Minister. When such instances could be cited from among the leaders of politics, it is not surprising that among the undistinguished Members corruption was notorious.[1]

Lecky says, also, of the same period:

The magistrates were in many cases not only notoriously ignorant and inefficient, but also what was termed " trading justices," men of whom Fielding said that " they were never indifferent in a cause but when they could get nothing on either side." The daring and the number of robbers increased till London hardly resembled a civilized town. " Thieves and robbers," said Smollett, speaking of 1730, " were now become more desperate and savage than they had ever appeared since mankind were civilized." The mayor and aldermen of London in 1744 drew up an address to the King, in which they stated that " divers confederacies of great numbers of evil-disposed persons, armed with bludgeons, pistols, cutlasses, and other dangerous weapons, infest not only the private lanes and passages, but likewise the public streets and places of usual concourse, and commit most daring outrages upon the persons of Your Majesty's good subjects whose affairs oblige them to pass through the streets, by robbing and wounding them, and these acts are frequently perpetrated at such times as were heretofore deemed hours of security." . . . The more experienced robbers for a time completely overawed the authorities. " Officers of justice," wrote Fielding, " have owned to me that they have passed by such, with warrants in their pockets against them, without daring to apprehend them; and, indeed, they could not be blamed for not exposing themselves to sure destruction; for it is a melancholy truth that at this very day a rogue no sooner gives the alarm within certain purlieus than twenty or thirty armed villains are found ready to come to his assistance."

[1] *A History of England in the Eighteenth Century,* William Edward Hartpole Lecky. Vol. I, p. 393.

At the same period the country roads of England were beset by highwaymen. Dick Turpin, Jonathan Wild, and Jack Shepard shared the admiration and sympathy of the people with the daring smugglers who waged continual war on all the coasts against the collectors of the government revenue. The customs of the country permitted, and the laws did not prevent, the plundering of all wrecks upon the coasts. The jails were filthy breeding places of pestilence. There was but little systematic effort for the relief of the insane, the diseased, the injured, or those helpless through infancy or age; and there was but little effort toward education or enlightenment outside of the fortunate few who made up the landed aristocracy.

When we reflect that these conditions existed so late as during the lives of the men who signed the American Declaration of Independence, and draw a comparison with the conditions existing today through the development of the same political institutions, under the control of the same race, in England, in the United States, in Canada and Australia, we cannot fail to realize that the evolution of self-government has been accompanied by amazing progress, not only in material prosperity, but in honesty, in humanity, and in the capacity to maintain order and do justice that leads to the higher intellectual and spiritual life of mankind.

In our own country we may take for comparison the shameful breach of the terms of Burgoyne's surrender, the refusal of the States to give effect to the provisions of the treaty of peace with England for the protection of the loyalists; the impotence of the Continental Congress, which Charles Lee described as "a stable of stupid cattle that stumbled at every step"; the jealousies, the pettiness, and the narrow prejudice that hampered and almost ruined the work of Washington; the incapacity of administration to which, and not to poverty, was due the distress at Valley Forge, where the footsteps of our poor soldiers could be traced by the blood on the snow, not because there were no shoes and stockings, but because shoes and stockings were not delivered where they were needed.

The humiliating experience of the second war with England revealed inefficiency and incompetency of federal administration that would be ludicrous if it were not lamentable.

It would not be possible now to elect such a man as Aaron Burr vice-president of the United States; or to leave in command of the army a man like Wilkinson, who was known to be in receipt of an annual payment of two thousand dollars from Spain while we were in controversy with that country over the possession of Florida, and whose friends defended him by the assertion that while he took the money he did not mean to give Spain any equivalent for it.

Such a condition of affairs as prevailed in our Congress at the time of the *Crédit Mobilier* business could not exist now. The atmosphere which existed in Washington at that time made it possible for a group of men, most distinguished and powerful among the public servants of the nation, to purchase or accept gifts of securities of corporations upon whose interests they were to vote in one or the other House of Congress. The whole tone of the public service was such that their moral vision was obscured. The same men today would find it impossible to do what they did then, because there is a clearer air and a better recognized standard of official morality. The conditions which made it possible for the unfortunate Belknap, as Secretary of War, to sell appointments, and for the trusted official aides of the President to be smirched by the whisky frauds of Grant's second administration, happily no longer exist, and no longer can exist.

The very nature of the evils which we are now most earnestly calling upon the Government to remedy is an evidence of the advance in governmental ethics and efficiency, for those evils consist very largely of practices which formerly passed unnoticed, while still greater evils engrossed the efforts for reform.

A fair illustration of this is to be found in an old statute of the state of New York. It is entitled " An Act instituting a lottery for the promotion of literature and for other purposes," passed April 13, 1814. It begins:

WHEREAS, Well-regulated seminaries of learning are of immense importance to every country, and tend especially, by the diffusion of science and the promotion of morals, to defend and perpetuate the liberties of a free state: Therefore,

SECTION 1. *Be it enacted by the People of the State of New York, represented in Senate and Assembly,* That there shall be raised by lottery, in successive classes, a sum equal in amount to the several appropriations made by this act.

The act then proceeds to appropriate the sum of one hundred thousand dollars for the benefit of Union College, forty thousand dollars for the benefit of Hamilton College, forty thousand dollars for the Asbury African Church in the city of New York for the purpose of enabling them to discharge a debt and to establish a school, and thirty thousand dollars for the College of Physicians and Surgeons; and it makes certain provisions for the benefit of Columbia College.

There was a tradition among American college men in my youth that old Doctor Eliphalet Nott — *clarum et venerabile nomen* — bought out the interests of the other institutions under this statute and made much money for Union College out of the lottery, doubtless greatly to " the diffusion of science and the promotion of morals."

I have often thought in recent years, when I have seen very good people wringing their hands over the failure of government to wholly suppress gambling in its various forms, that a reference to this standard of the year 1814 showed the difficulty to be, not the decadence of government, but the coal lands — have awakened intense indignation among the defendants and their friends, because the wrong was so inveterate that they had come to look upon it as a right. For more than a generation it had been regarded as a natural and unobjectionable thing to get possession of the public land by hook or by crook; and when the officers of the law presented and enforced the novel idea that it was as dishonest to deprive the Government of its land illegally as to deprive an individual of his land illegally, it seemed a cruel injustice. There was simply a little advance of the moral standard which gave life to laws that had been dead before. The whole system of the Federal Government has been lifted up to a higher plane of clearer moral vision, just as the whole system of British administration has been lifted up since the corrupt days of Walpole.

The elective franchise has become a more honest expression of popular will. Only men who are now growing old can remember, and history has not yet adequately recorded, the gross frauds, the tricks and devices, and acts of violence which prevented fair elections forty-odd years ago, before the federal election laws of 1870 and 1871 — laws which have passed out of existence, but have left their impress upon the legislation of the States of the Union. In those days, before there was any registration of voters, the wayfaring man could vote the resident out of house and home, and the count of votes was at the mercy of anybody who could succeed in buying a local election officer. The ballots with which to vote were furnished only by the local party organization, and were printed and folded and bunched and distributed by the workers of each party. I have known the voters of a congressional district to go to the polls on election day and find all the congressional ballots distributed for one candidate, and none to be obtained for the other candidate, because the local leader on one side had been bought by the other side. I have seen a file of men marched out of a tramp lodging house with their ballots held aloft in one hand continuously in plain sight until they had deposited them in the ballot box, in order to give the necessary evidence that they were voting according to the contract under which they were immediately thereafter to be paid. Now, the system of registration and the revision of the registry lists are substantially effective to confine voting to the qualified voters. The ballot is furnished by the state; the method of voting upon the Australian ballot in all its forms, by marking it in secret, makes bribery uncertain and unprofitable, because it is impossible to tell how any one votes, and the man who would take money for his vote cannot be depended upon to vote as he has agreed. Both the voting and the counting are protected by adequate supervision and full opportunity for watchers in the interest of the candidates and of the different parties. The change from dishonest and unfair elections to honest and fair elections is fundamental to the successful working of popular government and is in the course of ordinary and natural political development. It is the same kind of change which has taken place in England since the days before the Reform Bill of 1832; and that it is permanently effective we may be sure, because it is the natural course of political development here, as it has been in England.

I need not describe the growth, the maintenance, the systematic regulation, and efficiency of public and private charities, of public and private institutions for education, for the diffusion of knowledge, for the prosecution of scientific research and experiment, and for the encouragement of art — the enormous sums of money applied to these purposes, the active and unwearying efforts of multitudes of men and women devoted to them; for these are a part of the daily life of every American community. They show an advance in public intelligence and moral qualities working through that associated effort which is essential to government, and to which government is essential; and they justify the expectation of continued advancement in the future.

The fact that American popular government now has serious and difficult questions to deal with is no just cause for distrust. Government always has difficult questions to deal with, and we are assured by the advance already made of democracy's competency in the future. The great questions of capital and labor, of concentrated corporate wealth, and of diffused and general well-being, are merely natural incidents to progress.

The inventions and discoveries of the last century, the applications of science to useful arts, have enormously increased the productive power and therefore the wealth of mankind. By the use of machinery and newly devised processes the same number of men can produce, in manufacture and in agriculture, a far greater quantity and variety of the objects which contribute to the necessities, the comfort, and the pleasures of man than in former years. Unsuspected riches of the earth have been revealed and appropriated. Facilities for transportation have given a value to products which would once have been worthless because not needed at the point of production and not available for use elsewhere.

We are now witnessing the natural and inevitable struggle for a fair division of this new and rapidly increasing wealth. The ideal distribution would be that the inventor and discoverer, the organizing and directing intelligence and energy, should have a fair share for their contribution; that the capitalist should have a fair share for the use of his money and the risk which he incurs, measured by the chances of loss which so frequently turn against him; that the wage-worker should have his fair share in increase of wages and

THE CITIZEN'S PART IN GOVERNMENT 71

decrease in hours of labor, because he produces so much more by his labor than he formerly did; and that the consumers should have their fair share in decrease of price of the objects which are produced with so much less expense and effort.

It is inevitable that each one of these classes should differ from all the others as to the share to which it is entitled, and that there should be a continual struggle between them in the process of adjustment leading to a fair division. That process and that struggle will continue so long as wealth continues to increase.

One inevitable incident of this process is that at the outset some of these classes will get more than their share, and these are usually the organizer and the capitalist, because they have the advantage of initial position in respect of each new increment of wealth; so that the struggle ordinarily takes the form of demands by the wage-workers and the consumers to increase their shares of the new wealth at the expense of the capitalists and the organizers. Another incident of the process is that the laws framed to meet one set of conditions are constantly being found to need modification in order to insure just distribution of wealth and just rewards of intelligence, skill, and industry under the new conditions brought about by industrial progress. We are constantly finding that laws formerly adequate, when applied to new conditions permit some men to get lawfully more than is fair, while others cannot get lawfully as much as their fair share out of the industrial activity to which the whole community contributes in varying ways and degrees. For example, the laws relating to corporate organization, capitalization, consolidation, reorganization, and extension, which formerly served their purpose very well, are now seen to make it possible for some men who get into corporate control to make enormous fortunes without apparently violating any law, but for which they render really no return whatever to the wealth of the community. Morally, the action of these men does not necessarily differ in kind from the action which always has prevailed in the business world, where men determine the price of their commodities rather by what they will bring in the market than by any estimate of the good they will do the purchasers. But these great transactions call attention sharply to the fact that the legal rules governing corporate business require to be changed so that unconscionable advantages cannot be lawfully obtained; and moreover such transactions are often accompanied by such suppressions of full information and disregard of fiduciary obligations as to show that the law needs to be strengthened in those directions.

The facilities of transportation and communication which enable modern business to spread over a great expanse of territory have made it possible for so-called trusts and combinations to be made for the purpose of driving out competitors, restricting production and increasing prices, for which the old and simple rules designed to prevent engrossing, forestalling, and regrating in the English rural community are quite inadequate; and new laws and new agencies for their enforcement are necessary to accomplish the same results.

On the other hand, labor organizations, designed for the just purpose of securing fair treatment as to employment, wages, and hours and conditions of work, are on their part endeavoring to put up prices, restrict production, and drive out competition by stringent rules which prohibit any member from doing more than a specified amount of work each day under penalty of expulsion, and which prohibit the employment of any one not a member of the union under penalty of a strike.

All of these things are but incidents of the process of adjustment in the division of the new wealth; some of them come from attempts to get what is fair and some of them from attempts to get more than is fair. Our popular government is dealing with them assiduously, by awakened public opinion gradually crystallizing into laws adapted to meet the new conditions. This process involves no new principles, but merely the adaptation of the same old principles of law with which our fathers were familiar. The things which are happening and the necessity for continual reform of law and administration argue no decline in business morality and no inadequacy of our political system to continue its efficacy and its improvement.

There is occasionally undue excitement; but it is temporary, and whenever it is seen to approach the verge of destructive action it is promptly calmed and restrained by the sober judgment of the people.

Some workingmen's associations hold meetings where violent speeches are made and carry red flags in processions; but so far, whenever a square issue is raised among any great and widespread body of laboring men between anarchy and socialism on one side and the principles which underlie the American social and industrial system on the other, the decision is in favor of good Americanism. The Secretary of Commerce and Labor informs me that within the last dozen years the percentage of socialists in the labor organizations of the United States has decreased from about thirty-three per cent to about eight per cent. I do not know to what extent this has been by change within the labor organizations, or to what extent by separation of socialists from the organizations. However it has come about it indicates that so far the sober judgment of the great mass of the wage-workers of the United States is in favor of the conditions of their present prosperity as against socialism.

In considering the efficiency of democratic institutions we must remember the millions of immigrants who have its progress or its decadence, depends upon all of us, and it depends upon each one of us.

I commend to you as a guide to your duty of citizenship these words of Lecky, the historian — not a rhetorician, but a discriminating and thoughtful student:

> All civic virtue, all the heroism and self-sacrifice of patriotism spring ultimately from the habit men acquire of regarding their nation as a great organic whole, identifying themselves with its fortunes in the past as in the present, and looking forward anxiously to its future destinies. When the members of any nation have come to regard their country as nothing more than the plot of ground on which they reside, and their government as a mere organization for providing police or contracting treaties; when they have ceased to entertain any warmer feelings for one another than those which private interest, or personal friendship, or a mere general philanthropy, may produce, the moral dissolution of that nation is at hand. Even in the order of material interests the well-being of each generation is in a great degree dependent upon the forbearance, self-sacrifice, and providence of those who have preceded it, and civic virtues can never flourish in a generation which thinks only of itself.

EXPERIMENTS IN GOVERNMENT
AND
THE ESSENTIALS
OF THE CONSTITUTION

from the mere union of states towards the union of individuals in the relation of national citizenship.

The same causes have greatly reduced the independence of personal and family life. In the eighteenth century life was simple. The producer and consumer were near together and could find each other. Every one who had an equivalent to give in property or service could readily secure the support of himself and his family without asking anything from government except the preservation of order. Today almost all Americans are dependent upon the action of a great number of other persons mostly unknown. About half of our people are crowded into the cities and large towns. Their food, clothes, fuel, light, water — all come from distant sources, of which they are in the main ignorant, through a vast, complicated machinery of production and distribution with which they have little direct relation. If anything occurs to interfere with the working of the machinery, the consumer is individually helpless. To be certain that he and his family may continue to live he must seek the power of combination with others, and in the end he inevitably calls upon that great combination of all citizens which we call government to do something more than merely keep the peace — to regulate the machinery of production and distribution and safeguard it from interference so that it shall continue to work.

A similar change has taken place in the conditions under which a great part of our people engage in the industries by which they get their living. Under comparatively simple industrial conditions the relation between employer and employee was mainly a relation of individual to individual with individual freedom of contract and freedom of opportunity essential to equality in the commerce of life. Now, in the great manufacturing, mining and transportation industries of the country, instead of the free give and take of individual contract there is substituted a vast system of collective bargaining between great masses of men organized and acting through their representatives, or the individual on the one side accepts what he can get from superior power on the other. In the movement of these mighty forces of organization the individual laborer, the individual stockholder, the individual consumer, is helpless.

There has been another change of conditions through the development of political organization. The theory of political activity which had its origin approximately in the administration of President Jackson, and which is characterized by Marcy's declaration that " to the victors belong the spoils," tended to make the possession of office the primary and all-absorbing purpose of political conflict. A complicated system of party organization and representation grew up under which a disciplined body of party workers in each state supported each other, controlled the machinery of nomination, and thus controlled nominations. The members of state legislatures and other officers, when elected, felt a more acute responsibility to the organization which could control their renomination than to the electors, and therefore became accustomed to shape their conduct according to the wishes of the nominating organization. Accordingly the real power of government came to be vested to a high degree in these unofficial political organizations, and where there was a strong man at the head of an organization his control came to be something very closely approaching dictatorship. Another feature of this system aggravated its evils. As population grew, political campaigns became more expensive. At the same time, as wealth grew, corporations for production and transportation increased in capital and extent of operations and became more dependent upon the protection or toleration of government. They found a ready means to secure this by contributing heavily to the campaign funds of political organizations, and therefore their influence played a large part in determining who should be nominated and elected to office. So that in many states political organizations controlled the operations of government, in accordance with the wishes of the managers of the great corporations. Under these circumstances our governmental institutions were not working as they were intended to work, and a desire to break up and get away from this extra constitutional method of controlling our constitutional government has caused a great part of the new political methods of the last few years.

It is manifest that the laws which were entirely adequate, under the conditions of a century ago, to secure individual and public welfare must be in many respects inadequate to accomplish the same results under all these new conditions; and our people are now engaged in the difficult but imperative duty of adapting their laws to the life of today. The changes in conditions have come very rapidly and a good deal of experiment will be necessary to find out just what government can do and ought to do to meet them.

The process of devising and trying new laws to meet new conditions naturally leads to the question whether we need not merely to make new laws but also to modify the principles upon which our government is based and the institutions of government designed for the application of those principles to the affairs of life. Upon this question it is of the utmost importance that we proceed with considerate wisdom.

By institutions of government I mean the established rule or order of action through which the sovereign (in our case the sovereign people) attains the ends of government. The governmental institutions of Great Britain have been established by the growth through many centuries of a great body of accepted rules and customs which, taken together, are called the British Constitution. In this country we have set forth in the Declaration of Independence the principles which we consider to lie at the basis of civil society: " that all men are created equal, that they are endowed by their Creator with certain unalienable Rights, that among these are Life, Liberty and the pursuit of Happiness. That to secure these rights, Governments are instituted among Men, deriving their just powers from the consent of the governed."

In our federal and state constitutions we have established the institutions through which these rights are to be secured. We have declared what officers shall make the laws, what officers shall execute them, what officers shall sit in judgment upon claims of right under them. We have prescribed how these officers shall be selected and the tenure by which they shall hold their offices. We have limited them in the powers which they are to exercise, and, where it has been deemed necessary, we have imposed specific duties upon them. The body of rules thus prescribed constitute the governmental institutions of the United States.

When proposals are made to change these institutions there are certain general considerations which should be observed.

The first consideration is that free government is impossible except through prescribed and established governmental institutions, which work out the ends of government through many separate human agents, each doing his part in obedience to law. Popular will cannot execute itself directly except through a mob. Popular will cannot get itself executed through an irresponsible executive, for that is simple autocracy. An executive limited only by the direct expression of popular will cannot be held to responsibility against his will, because, having possession of all the powers of government, he can prevent any true, free, and general expression adverse to himself, and unless he yields voluntarily he can be overturned only by a revolution. The familiar Spanish-American dictatorships are illustrations of this. A dictator once established by what is or is alleged to be public choice never permits an expression of public will which will displace him, and he goes out only through a new revolution because he alone controls the machinery through which he could be displaced peaceably. A system with a plebiscite at one end and Louis Napoleon at the other could not give France free government; and it was only after the humiliation of defeat in a great war and the horrors of the Commune that the French people were able to establish a government which would really execute their will through carefully devised institutions in which they gave their chief executive very little power indeed.

We should, therefore, reject every proposal which involves the idea that the people can rule merely by voting, or merely by voting and having one man or group of men to execute their will.

A second consideration is that in estimating the value of any system of governmental institutions due regard must be had to the true functions of government and to the limitations imposed by nature upon what it is possible for government to accomplish. We all know of course that we cannot abolish all the evils in this world by statute or by the enforcement of statutes, nor can we prevent the inexorable law of nature which decrees that suffering shall follow vice, and all the evil passions and folly of mankind. Law cannot give to depravity the rewards of virtue, to indolence the rewards of industry, to indifference the rewards of ambition, or to ignorance the rewards of learning. The utmost that government can do is measurably to protect men, not against the wrong they do themselves but against wrong done by others, and to promote the long, slow process of educating mind and character to a better knowledge and nobler standards of life and conduct. We know all this, but when we see how much misery there is in the world and instinctively cry out against it, and when we see some things that government may do to mitigate it, we are apt to forget how little after all it is possible for any government to do, and to hold the particular government of the time and place to a standard of responsibility which no government can possibly meet. The chief motive power which has moved mankind along the course of development which we call the progress of civilization has been the sum total of intelligent selfishness in a vast number of individuals, each working for his own support, his own gain, his own betterment. It is that which has cleared the forests and cultivated the fields and built the ships and railroads, made the discoveries and inventions, covered the earth with commerce, softened by intercourse the enmities of nations and races, and made possible the wonders of literature and of art. Gradually, during the long process, selfishness has grown more intelligent, with a broader view of individual benefit from the common good, and gradually the influences of nobler standards of altruism, of justice, and human sympathy have impressed themselves upon the conception of right conduct among civilized men. But the complete control of such motives will be the millennium. Any attempt to enforce a millennial standard now by law must necessarily fail, and any judgment which assumes government's responsibility to enforce such a standard must be an unjust judgment. Indeed, no such standard can ever be forced. It must come, not by superior force, but from the changed nature of man, from his willingness to be altogether just and merciful.

A third consideration is that it is not merely useless but injurious for government to attempt too much. It is manifest that to enable it to deal with the new conditions I have described we must invest government with authority to interfere with the individual conduct of the citizen to a

Every one of these five characteristics of the government established by the Constitution was a distinct advance beyond the ancient attempts at popular government, and the elimination of any one of them would be a retrograde movement and a reversion to a former and discarded type of government. In each case it would be the abandonment of a distinctive feature of government which has succeeded, in order to go back and try again the methods of government which have failed. Of course we ought not to take such a backward step except under the pressure of inevitable necessity.

The first two of the characteristics which I have enumerated, those which embrace the conception of representative government and the conception of individual liberty, were the products of the long process of development of freedom in England and America. They were not invented by the makers of the Constitution. They have been called inventions of the Anglo-Saxon race. They are the chief contributions of that race to the political development of civilization.

The expedient of representation first found its beginning in the Saxon *witenagemot*. It was lost in the Norman conquest. It was restored step by step, through the centuries in which Parliament established its power as an institution through the granting or withholding of aids and taxes for the king's use. It was brought to America by the English colonists. It was the practice of the colonies which formed the Federal Union. It entered into the Constitution as a matter of course, because it was the method by which modern liberty had been steadily growing stronger and broader for six centuries as opposed to the direct, unrepresentative method of government in which the Greek and Roman and Italian republics had failed. This representative system has in its turn impressed itself upon the nations which derived their political ideas from Rome, and has afforded the method through which popular liberty has been winning forward in its struggle against royal and aristocratic power and privilege the world over. Bluntschli, the great Heidelberg publicist of the last century, says:

> Representative government and self-government are the great works of the English and American peoples. The English have produced representative monarchy with parliamentary legislation and parliamentary government. The Americans have produced the representative republic. We Europeans upon the Continent recognize in our turn that in representative government alone lies the hoped-for union between civil order and popular liberty.[1]

The initiative and compulsory referendum are attempts to cure the evils which have developed in our practice of representative government by means of a return to the old, unsuccessful, and discarded method of direct legislation and by rehabilitating one of the most impracticable of Rousseau's theories. Every candid student of our governmental affairs must agree that the evils to be cured have been real and that the motive which has prompted the proposal of the initiative and referendum is commendable. I do not think that these expedients will prove wise or successful ways of curing these evils for reasons which I will presently indicate; but it is not necessary to assume that their trial will be destructive of our system of government. They do not aim to destroy representative government, but to modify and control it, and were it not that the effect of these particular methods is likely to go beyond the intention of their advocates they would not interfere seriously with representative government except in so far as they might ultimately prove to be successful expedients. If they did not work satisfactorily they would be abandoned, leaving representative government still in full force and effectiveness.

[1] J. C. Bluntschli's Introduction to the *Miscellaneous Writings of Francis Lieber*, Vol. II, p. 12.

practicable. There always will be, and if the direct system is to amount to anything there must be, many proposals urged upon the voters at each opportunity.

The measures submitted at one time in some of the western states now fill considerable volumes.

With each proposal the voter's task becomes more complicated and difficult.

Yet our ballots are already too complicated. The great blanket sheets with scores of officers and hundreds of names to be marked are quite beyond the intelligent action in detail of nine men out of ten.

The most thoughtful reformers are already urging that the voter's task be made more simple by giving him fewer things to consider and act upon at the same time.

This is the substance of what is called the Short Ballot reform; and it is right, for the more questions divide public attention the fewer questions the voters really decide for themselves on their own judgment and the greater the power of the professional politician.

There is moreover a serious danger to be apprehended from the attempt at legislation by the initiative and compulsory referendum, arising from its probable effect on the character of representative bodies. These expedients result from distrust of legislatures. They are based on the assertion that the people are not faithfully represented in their legislative bodies, but are misrepresented. The same distrust has led to the encumbering of modern state constitutions by a great variety of minute limitations upon legislative power. Many of these constitutions, instead of being simple framework of government, are bulky and detailed statutes legislating upon subjects which the people are unwilling to trust the legislature to deal with. So between the new constitutions, which exclude the legislatures from power, and the referendum, by which the people overrule what they do, and the initiative, by which the people legislate in their place, the legislative representatives who were formerly honored, are hampered, shorn of power, relieved of responsibility, discredited, and treated as unworthy of confidence. The unfortunate effect of such treatment upon the character of legislatures and the kind of men who will be willing to serve in them can well be imagined. It is the influence of such treatment that threatens representative institutions in our country. Granting that there have been evils in our legislative system which ought to be cured, I cannot think that this is the right way to cure them. It would seem that the true way is for the people of the country to address themselves to the better performance of their own duty in selecting their legislative representatives and in holding those representatives to strict responsibility for their action. The system of direct nominations, which is easy of application in the simple proceeding of selecting members of a legislature, and the short ballot reform aim at accomplishing that result. I think that along these lines the true remedy is to be found. No system of self-government will continue successful unless the voters have sufficient public spirit to perform their own duty at the polls, and the attempt to reform government by escaping from the duty of selecting honest and capable representatives, under the idea that the same voters who fail to perform that duty will faithfully perform the far more onerous and difficult duty of legislation, seems an exhibition of weakness rather than of progress.

II

ESSENTIALS OF THE CONSTITUTION

In the first of these lectures I specified certain essential characteristics of our system of government, and discussed the preservation of the first — its representative character. The four other characteristics specified have one feature in common. They all aim to preserve rights by limiting power.

Of these the most fundamental is the preservation in our Constitution of the Anglo-Saxon idea of individual liberty. The republics of Greece and Rome had no such conception. All political ideas necessarily concern man as a social animal, as a member of society — a member of the state. The ancient republics, however, put the state first and regarded the individual only as a member of the state. They had in view the public rights of the state in which all its members shared, and the rights of the members as parts of the whole, but they did not think of individuals as having rights independent of the state, or against the state. They never escaped from the attitude towards public and individual civil rights, which was dictated by the original and ever-present necessity of military organization and defense.

The Anglo-Saxon idea, on the other hand, looked first to the individual. In the early days of English history, without theorizing much upon the subject, the Anglo-Saxons began to work out their political institutions along the line expressed in our Declaration of Independence, that the individual citizen has certain inalienable rights — the right to life, to liberty, to the pursuit of happiness, and that government is not the source of these rights, but is the instrument for the preservation and promotion of them. So when a century and a half after the Conquest the barons of England set themselves to limit the power of the crown they did not demand a grant of rights. They asserted the rights of individual freedom and demanded observance of them, and they laid the corner stone of our system of government in this solemn pledge of the Great Charter:

> No freeman shall be taken, or imprisoned, or be disseized of his freehold, or his liberties, or his free customs, or be outlawed, or exiled, or otherwise destroyed, but by the lawful judgment of his peers, or by the law of the land.

Again and again in the repeated confirmations of the Great Charter, in the Petition of Rights, in the Habeas Corpus Act, in the Bill of Rights, in the Massachusetts Body of Liberties, in the Virginia Bill of Rights, and, finally, in the immortal Declaration of 1776 — in all the great utterances of striving for broader freedom which have marked the development of modern liberty, sounds the same dominant note of insistence upon the inalienable right of individual manhood under government but independent of government, and, if need be, against government, to life and liberty.

It is impossible to overestimate the importance of the consequences which followed from these two distinct and opposed theories of government. The one gave us the dominion, but also the decline and fall, of Rome. It followed the French Declaration of the Rights of Man, with the negation of those rights in the oppression of the Reign of Terror, the despotism of Napoleon, the popular submission to the Second Empire and the subservience of the individual citizen to official superiority which still prevails so widely on the continent of Europe. The tremendous potency of the other subdued the victorious Normans to the conquered Saxon's conception of justice, rejected the claims of divine right by the Stuarts, established capacity for self-government upon the independence of individual character that knows no superior but the law, and supplied the amazing formative power which has moulded, according to the course and practice of the common law, the thought and custom of the hundred millions of men drawn from all lands and all races who inhabit this continent north of the Rio Grande.

The mere declaration of a principle, however, is of little avail unless it be supported by practical and specific rules of conduct through which the principle shall receive effect. So Magna Charta imposed specific limitations upon royal authority to the end that individual liberty might be preserved, and so to the same end our Declaration of Independence was followed by those great rules of right conduct which we call the limitations of the Constitution. Magna Charta imposed its limitations upon the kings of England and all their officers and agents. Our Constitution imposed its limitations upon the sovereign people and all their officers and agents, excluding all the agencies of popular government from authority to do the particular things which would destroy or impair the declared inalienable right of the individual.

Thus the Constitution provides: No law shall be made by Congress prohibiting the free exercise of religion, or abridging the freedom of speech or of the press. The right of the people to keep and bear arms shall not be infringed. The right of the people to be secure in their persons, houses, papers, and effects, against unreasonable searches and seizures, shall not be violated. No person shall be subject for the same offense to be twice put in jeopardy of life or limb; nor be compelled, in any criminal case, to be a witness against himself; nor be deprived of life, liberty, or property without due process of law; nor shall private property be taken for public use without just compensation. In all criminal prosecutions, the accused shall enjoy the right to a speedy and public trial, by an impartial jury of the state and district wherein the crime shall have been committed; and to be informed of the nature and cause of the accusation, to

ESSENTIALS OF THE CONSTITUTION

be confronted with the witnesses against him, to have compulsory process for obtaining witnesses in his favor, and to have the assistance of counsel for his defense. Excessive bail shall not be required, nor excessive fines imposed, nor cruel and unusual punishment inflicted. The privilege of the writ of habeas corpus shall not be suspended, except in case of rebellion or invasion. No bill of attainder or *ex post facto* law shall be passed. And by the Fourteenth Amendment, no state shall deprive any person of life, liberty, or property, without due process of law; nor deny to any person within its jurisdiction the equal protection of the law.

We have lived so long under the protection of these rules that most of us have forgotten their importance. They have been unquestioned in America so long that most of us have forgotten the reasons for them. But if we lose them we shall learn the reasons by hard experience. And we are in some danger of losing them, not all at once but gradually, by indifference.

As Professor Sohm says, "The greatest and most far-reaching revolutions in history are not consciously observed at the time of their occurrence."[1]

Every one of these provisions has a history. Every one stops a way through which the overwhelming power of government has oppressed the weak individual citizen, and may do so again if the way be opened. Such provisions as these are not mere commands. They withhold power. The instant any officer, of whatever kind or grade, transgresses them he ceases to act as an officer. The power of sovereignty no longer supports him. The majesty of the law no longer gives him authority. The shield of the law no longer protects him. He becomes a trespasser, a despoiler, a law-breaker, and all the machinery of the law may be set in

---

[1] *The Institutes*, by Rudolph Sohm, professor of German law in the University of Leipzig, translated by James Crawford Ledlie, 2d ed., Oxford, 1901, p. 42.

anything else, we pay deference to the law which he represents, but the personal relation is one of equality. Give to that officer, however, unlimited power, or power which we do not know to be limited, and the relation at once becomes that of an inferior to a superior. The inevitable result of such a relation long continued is to deprive the people of the country of the individual habit of independence. This may be observed in many of the countries of Continental Europe, where official persons are treated with the kind of deference, and exercise the kind of authority, which are appropriate only to the relations between superior and inferior.

So the Massachusetts Constitution of 1780, after limiting the powers of each department to its own field, declares that this is done " to the end it may be a government of laws and not of men."

The third class of limitations I have mentioned are those made necessary by the novel system which I have described as superimposing upon a federation of state governments, a national government acting directly upon the individual citizens of the states. This expedient was wholly unknown before the adoption of our Constitution. All the confederations which had been attempted before that time were simply leagues of states, and whatever central authority there was derived its authority from and had its relations with the states as separate bodies politic. This was so of the old confederation. Each citizen owed his allegiance to his own state and each state had its obligations to the confederation. Under our constitutional system in every part of the territory of every state there are two sovereigns, and every citizen owes allegiance to both sovereigns — to his state and to his nation. In regard to some matters, which may generally be described as local, the state is supreme. In regard to other matters, which may generally be described as national, the nation is supreme. It is plain that to maintain the line between these two sovereignties operating in the same territory and upon the same citizens is a matter of no little difficulty and delicacy. Nothing has involved more constant discussion in our political history than questions of conflict between these two powers and we fought the great Civil War to determine the question whether in case of conflict the allegiance to the state or the allegiance to the nation was of superior obligation. We should observe that the Civil War arose because the Constitution did not draw a clear line between the national and state powers regarding slavery. It is of very great importance that both of these authorities, state and national, shall be preserved together and that the limitations which keep each within its proper province shall be maintained. If the power of the states were to override the power of the nation we should ultimately cease to have a nation and become only a body of really separate, although confederated, state sovereignties continually forced apart by diverse interests and ultimately quarreling with each other and separating altogether. On the other hand, if the power of the nation were to override that of the states and usurp their functions we should have this vast country, with its great population, inhabiting widely separated regions, differing in climate, in production, in industrial and social interests and ideas, governed in all its local affairs by one all-powerful, central government at Washington, imposing upon the home life and behavior of each community the opinions and ideas of propriety of distant majorities. Not only would this be intolerable and alien to the idea of free self-government, but it would be beyond the power of a central government to do directly. Decentralization would be made necessary by the mass of government business to be transacted, and so our separate localities would come to be governed by delegated authority — by proconsuls authorized from Washington to execute the will of the great majority of the whole people.

No one can doubt that this also would lead by its different route to the separation of our Union. Preservation of our dual system of government, carefully restrained in each of its parts by the limitations of the Constitution, has made possible our growth in local self-government and national power in the past, and, so far as we can see, it is essential to the continuance of that government in the future.

All of these three classes of constitutional limitations are therefore necessary to the perpetuity of our government. I do not wish to be understood as saying that every single limitation is essential. There are some limitations that might be changed and something different substituted. But the system of limitation must be continued if our governmental system is to continue — if we are not to lose the fundamental principles of government upon which our Union is maintained and upon which our race has won the liberty secured by law for which it has stood foremost in the world.

Lincoln covered this subject in one of his comprehensive statements that cannot be quoted too often. He said in the first inaugural:

> A majority held in restraint by constitutional checks and limitations and always changing easily with deliberate changes of popular opinion and sentiment is the only true sovereign of a free people. Whoever rejects it does of necessity fly to anarchy or despotism.

Rules of limitation, however, are useless unless they are enforced. The reason for restraining rules arises from a tendency to do the things prohibited. Otherwise no rule would be needed. Against all practical rules of limitation — all rules limiting official conduct, there is a constant pressure from one side or the other. Honest differences of opinion as to the extent of power, arising from different points of view make this inevitable, to say nothing of those weaknesses and faults of human nature which lead men to press the exercise of power to the utmost under the influence of ambition, of impatience with opposition to their designs, of selfish interest and the arrogance of office. No mere paper rules will restrain these powerful and common forces of human nature. The agency by which, under our system of government, observance of constitutional limitation is enforced is the judicial power. The Constitution provides that "This Constitution, and the laws of the United States which shall be made in pursuance thereof, and all treaties made, or which shall be made, under the authority of the United States, shall be the supreme law of the land; and the judges in every state shall be bound thereby, anything in the constitution or laws of any state to the contrary notwithstanding." Under this provision an enactment by Congress not made in pursuance of the Constitution, or an enactment of a state contrary to the Constitution, is not a law. Such an enactment should strictly have no more legal effect than the resolution of any private debating society. The Constitution also provides that the judicial power of the United States shall extend to all cases in law and equity arising under the Constitution and laws of the United States. Whenever, therefore, in a case before a federal court rights are asserted under or against some law which is claimed to violate some limitation of the Constitution the court is obliged to say whether the law does violate the Constitution or not, because if it does not violate the Constitution the court must give effect to it as law, while if it does violate the Constitution it is no law at all and the court is not at liberty to give effect to it. The courts do not render decisions like imperial rescripts declaring laws valid or invalid. They merely render judgment on the rights of the litigants in particular cases, and in arriving at their judgment they refuse to give effect to statutes which they find clearly not to be made in pursuance of the Constitution and therefore to be no laws at all. Their judgments are technically binding only in the particular case decided, but the knowledge that the court of last resort has reached such a conclusion concerning a statute, and that a similar conclusion would undoubtedly be reached in every case of an attempt to found rights upon the same statute, leads to a general acceptance of the invalidity of the statute.

There is only one alternative to having the courts decide upon the validity of legislative acts, and that is by requiring the courts to treat the opinion of the legislature upon the validity of its statutes, evidenced by their passage, as conclusive. But the effect of this would be that the legislature would not be limited at all except by its own will. All the provisions designed to maintain a government carried on by officers of limited powers, all the distinctions between what is permitted to the national government and what is permitted to the state governments, all the safeguards of the life, liberty and property of the citizen against arbitrary power, would cease to bind Congress, and on the same theory they would cease also to bind the legislatures of the states. Instead of the Constitution being superior to the laws the laws would be superior to the Constitution, and the essential principles of our government would disappear. More than one hundred years ago, Chief Justice Marshall, in the great case of Marbury v. Madison,[1] set forth the view upon which our government has ever since proceeded. He said:

> The powers of the legislature are defined and limited; and that those limits may not be mistaken or forgotten, the Constitution is written. To what purpose are powers limited, and to what purpose is that limitation committed to writing, if these limits may, at any time, be passed by those intended to be restrained ? The distinction between a government with limited and unlimited powers is abolished, if those limits do not confine the persons on whom they are imposed, and if acts prohibited and acts allowed are of equal obligation. It is a proposition too plain to be contested, that the Constitution controls any legislative act repugnant to it; or that the legislature may alter the Constitution by an ordinary act.

[1] 1 Cranch, pp. 137, 176–177.

Between these alternatives, there is no middle ground. The Constitution is either a superior, paramount law, unchangeable by ordinary means, or it is on a level with ordinary legislative acts, and, like other acts, is alterable when the legislature shall please to alter it. If the former part of the alternative be true, then a legislative act, contrary to the Constitution, is not law: if the latter part be true, then written constitutions are absurd attempts, on the part of the people, to limit a power, in its own nature illimitable.

Certainly, all those who have framed written constitutions contemplate them as forming the fundamental and paramount law of the nation, and consequently, the theory of every such government must be, that an act of the legislature, repugnant to the constitution, is void. This theory is essentially attached to a written constitution, and is, consequently, to be considered, by this court, as one of the fundamental principles of our society.

And of the same opinion was Montesquieu who gave the high authority of the *Esprit des lois* to the declaration that

There is no liberty if the power of judging be not separate from the legislative and executive powers; were it joined with the legislative the life and liberty of the subject would be exposed to arbitrary control.[1]

It is to be observed that the wit of man has not yet devised any better way of reaching a just conclusion as to whether a statute does or does not conflict with a constitutional limitation upon legislative power than the submission of the question to an independent and impartial court. The courts are not parties to the transactions upon which they pass. They are withdrawn by the conditions of their office from participation in business and political affairs out of which litigations arise. Their action is free from the chief dangers which threaten the undue extension of power, because, as Hamilton points out in *The Federalist*, they are the weakest branch of government: they neither hold the purse, as does the legislature, nor the sword, as does the executive. During all our history they have commanded and deserved the respect and confidence of the people. General acceptance

[1] *Esprit des lois*, by Charles Louis de Secondat Montesquieu, Vol. I, p. 181.

of their conclusions has been the chief agency in preventing here the discord and strife which afflict so many lands, and in preserving peace and order and respect for law.

Indeed in the effort to emasculate representative government to which I have already referred, the people of the experimenting states have greatly increased their reliance upon the courts. Every new constitution with detailed orders to the legislature is a forcible assertion that the people will not trust legislatures to determine the extent of their own powers, but will trust the courts.

Two of the new proposals in government which have been much discussed, directly relate to this system of constitutional limitations made effective through the judgment of the courts. One is the proposal for the recall of judges, and the other for the popular review of decisions, sometimes spoken of as the recall of decisions.

Under the first of these proposals, if a specified proportion of the voters are dissatisfied with a judge's decision they are empowered to require that at the next election, or at a special election called for that purpose, the question shall be presented to the electors whether the judge shall be permitted to continue in office or some other specified person shall be substituted in his place. This ordeal differs radically from the popular judgment which a judge is called upon to meet at the end of his term of office, however short that may be, because when his term has expired he is judged upon his general course of conduct while he has been in office and stands or falls upon that as a whole. Under the recall a judge may be brought to the bar of public judgment immediately upon the rendering of a particular decision which excites public interest and he will be subject to punishment if that decision is unpopular. Judges will naturally be afraid to render unpopular decisions. They will hear and decide cases with a stronger incentive to avoid condemnation themselves than to do justice to the litigant or the accused. Instead of independent and courageous judges we shall have timid and time-serving judges. That highest duty of the judicial power to extend the protection of the law to the weak, the friendless, the unpopular, will in a great measure fail. Indirectly the effect will be to prevent the enforcement of the essential limitations upon official power because the judges will be afraid to declare that there is a violation when the violation is to accomplish some popular object.

The recall of decisions aims directly at the same result. Under such an arrangement, if the courts have found a particular law to be a violation of one of the fundamental rules of limitation prescribed in the Constitution, and the public feeling of the time is in favor of disregarding that limitation in that case, an election is to be held, and if the people in that election vote that the law shall stand, it is to stand, although it be a violation of the Constitution; that is to say, if at any time a majority of the voters of a state (and ultimately the same would be true of the people of the United States) choose not to be bound in any particular case by the rule of right conduct which they have established for themselves, they are not to be bound. This is sometimes spoken of as a popular reversal of the decisions of courts. That I take to be an incorrect view. The power which would be exercised by the people under such an arrangement would be, not judicial, but legislative. The action would not be a decision that the court was wrong in finding a law unconstitutional, but it would be making a law valid which was invalid before because unconstitutional. In such an election the majority of the voters would make a law where no law had existed before; and they would make that law in violation of the rules of conduct by which the people themselves had solemnly declared they ought to be bound. The exercise of such a power, if it is to exist, cannot be limited to the particular cases which you or I or any man now living may have in mind. It must be general. If it can be exercised at all it can and will be exercised by the majority whenever they wish to exercise it. If it can be employed to make a workmen's compensation act in such terms as to violate the Constitution, it can be employed to prohibit the worship of an unpopular religious sect, or to take away the property of an unpopular rich man without compensation, or to prohibit freedom of speech and of the press in opposition to prevailing opinion, or to deprive one accused of crime of a fair trial when he has been condemned already by the newspapers. In every case the question whether the majority shall be bound by those general principles of action which the people have prescribed for themselves will be determined in that case by the will of the majority, and therefore in no case will the majority be bound except by its own will at the time.

The exercise of such a power would strike at the very foundation of our system of government. It would be a reversion to the system of the ancient republics where the state was everything and the individual nothing except as a part of the state, and where liberty perished. It would be a repudiation of the fundamental principle of Anglo-Saxon liberty which we inherit and maintain, for it is the very soul of our political institutions that they protect the individual against the majority. "All men," says the Declaration, "are endowed by their Creator with certain unalienable Rights." Governments are instituted to secure these rights. The rights are not derived from any majority. They are not disposable by any majority. They are superior to all majorities. The weakest minority, the most despised sect, exist by their own right. The most friendless and lonely human being on American soil holds his right to life and liberty and the pursuit of happiness, and all that goes to make them up, by title indefeasible against the world, and it is the glory of American self-government that by the limitations of the Constitution we have protected that right against even ourselves.

That protection cannot be continued and that right cannot be maintained, except by jealously preserving at all times and under all circumstances the rule of principle which is eternal over the will of majorities which shift and pass away.

Democratic absolutism is just as repulsive, and history has shown it to be just as fatal, to the rights of individual manhood as is monarchical absolutism.

But it is not necessary to violate the rules of action which we have established for ourselves in the Constitution in order to deal by law with the new conditions of the time, for these rules of action are themselves subject to popular control. If the rules are so stated that they are thought to prevent the doing of something which is not contrary to the principles of liberty but demanded by them, the true remedy is to be found in reconsidering what the rules ought to be and, if need be, in restating them so that they will give more complete effect to the principles they are designed to enforce. If, as I believe, there ought to be in my own state, for example, a workman's compensation act to supersede the present unsatisfactory system of accident litigation, and if the Constitution forbids such a law — which I very much doubt — the true remedy is not to cast to the winds all systematic self-restraint and to inaugurate a new system of doing whatever we please whenever we please, unrestrained by declared rules of conduct; but it is to follow the orderly and ordinary method of amending the Constitution so that the rule protecting the right to property shall not be so broadly stated as to prevent legislation which the principle underlying the rule demands.

The difference between the proposed practice of overriding the Constitution by a vote and amending the Constitution is vital. It is the difference between breaking a rule and making a rule; between acting without any rule in a particular case and determining what ought to be the rule of action applicable to all cases.

Our legislatures frequently try to evade constitutional provisions, and doubtless popular majorities seeking specific objects would vote the same way; but set the same people to consider what the fundamental law ought to be, and confront them with the question whether they will abandon in general the principles and the practical rules of conduct according to principles, upon which our government rests, and they will instantly refuse. While their minds are consciously and avowedly addressed to that subject they will stand firm for the general rules that will protect them and their children against oppression and usurpation, and they will change those rules only if need be to make them enforce more perfectly the principles which underlie them.

Communities, like individuals, will declare for what they believe to be just and right; but communities, like individuals, can be led away from their principles step by step under the temptations of specific desires and supposed expediencies until the principles are a dead letter and allegiance to them is a mere sham.

And that is the way in which popular governments lose their vitality and perish.

The Roman consuls derived their power from the people and were responsible to the people; but Rome went on pretending that the emperors and their servants were consuls long after the prætorians were the only source of power and the only power exercised was that of irresponsible despotism.

A number of countries have copied our Constitution coupled with a provision that the constitutional guarantees may be suspended in case of necessity. We are all familiar with the result. The guarantees of liberty and justice and order have been forgotten: the government is dictatorship and the popular will is expressed only by revolution.

Nor, so far as our national system is concerned has there yet appeared any reason to suppose that suitable laws to meet the new conditions cannot be enacted without either overriding or amending the Constitution. The liberty of contract and the right of private property which are protected by the limitations of the Constitution are held subject to the police power of government to pass and enforce laws for the protection of the public health, public morals, and public safety. The scope and character of the regulations required to accomplish these objects vary as the conditions of life in the country vary. Many interferences with contract and with property which would have been unjustifiable a century ago are demanded by the conditions which exist now and are permissible without violating any constitutional limitation. What will promote these objects the legislative power decides with large discretion, and the courts have no authority to review the exercise of that discretion. It is only when laws are passed under color of the police power and having no real or substantial relation to the purposes for which the power exists, that the courts can refuse to give them effect.

By a multitude of judicial decisions in recent years our courts have sustained the exercise of this vast and progressive power in dealing with the new conditions of life under a great variety of circumstances. The principal difficulty in sustaining the exercise of the power has been caused ordinarily by the fact that carelessly or ignorantly drawn statutes either have failed to exhibit the true relation between the regulation proposed and the object sought, or have gone farther than the attainment of the legitimate object justified. A very good illustration of this is to be found in the federal employer's liability act which was carelessly drawn and passed by Congress in 1906 and was declared unconstitutional by the Supreme Court, but which was carefully drawn and passed by Congress in 1908 and was declared constitutional by the same court.

Insistence upon hasty and violent methods rather than orderly and deliberate methods is really a result of impatience with the slow methods of true progress in popular government. We should probably make little progress were there not in every generation some men who, realizing evils, are eager for reform, impatient of delay, indignant at opposition, and intolerant of the long, slow processes by which the great body of the people may consider new proposals in all their relations, weigh their advantages and disadvantages, discuss their merits, and become educated either to their acceptance or rejection. Yet that is the method of progress in which no step, once taken, needs to be retraced; and it is the only way in which a democracy can avoid destroying its institutions by the impulsive substitution of novel and attractive but impracticable expedients.

The wisest of all the Fathers of the Republic has spoken, not for his own day alone but for all generations to come after him, in the solemn admonitions of the Farewell Address. It was to us that Washington spoke when he said:

> The basis of our political systems is the right of the people to make and to alter their constitutions of government; but the constitution which at any time exists, till changed by an explicit and authentic act of the whole people, is sacredly obligatory upon all. . . . Towards the preservation of your government, and the permanency of your present happy state, it is requisite, not only that you steadily discountenance irregular oppositions to its acknowledged authority but also that you resist with care the spirit of innovation upon its principles, however specious the pretexts. One method of assault may be to effect, in the forms of the constitution, alterations which will impair the energy of the system, and thus to undermine what cannot be directly overthrown. In all the changes to which you may be invited, remember that time and habit are at least as necessary to fix the true character of governments as of other human institutions; that experience is the surest standard by which to

test the real tendency of the existing constitution of a country; that facility in changes, upon the credit of mere hypothesis and opinion, exposes to perpetual changes, from the endless variety of hypothesis and opinion.

While, in the nature of things, each generation must assume the task of adapting the working of its government to new conditions of life as they arise, it would be the folly of ignorant conceit for any generation to assume that it can lightly and easily improve upon the work of the founders in those matters which are, by their nature, of universal application to the permanent relations of men in civil society.

Religion, the philosophy of morals, the teaching of history, the experience of every human life, point to the same conclusion — that in the practical conduct of life the most difficult and the most necessary virtue is self-restraint. It is the first lesson of childhood; it is the quality for which great monarchs are most highly praised; the man who has it not is feared and shunned; it is needed most where power is greatest; it is needed more by men acting in a mass than by individuals, because men in the mass are more irresponsible and difficult of control than individuals. The makers of our Constitution, wise and earnest students of history and of life, discerned the great truth that self-restraint is the supreme necessity and the supreme virtue of a democracy. The people of the United States have exercised that virtue by the establishment of rules of right action in what we call the limitations of the Constitution, and until this day they have rigidly observed those rules. The general judgment of students of government is that the success and permanency of the American system of government are due to the establishment and observance of such general rules of conduct. Let us change and adapt our laws as the shifting conditions of the times require, but let us never abandon or weaken this fundamental and essential characteristic of our ordered liberty.

THE first constitution of the state of New York was adopted on April 20, 1777. Since that date, the state has had three separate and distinct constitutions, and six constitutional conventions: 1801, 1821, 1846, 1867, 1894, and 1915. The second constitution, framed by the constitutional convention, was adopted in 1821. The third constitution, adopted in 1846, and ratified by the people, provided for a constitutional convention to be held every twenty years thereafter, and required the legislature to submit the question of holding a convention to a vote of the people. The convention of 1867 adopted a constitution, which was defeated at the polls. The Honorable David B. Hill, then governor, vetoed the bill providing for a constitutional convention in 1887. In 1894, the fifth constitutional convention drafted various amendments to the constitution, and the constitution as thus amended was submitted to and approved by the people. The sixth constitutional convention, held in 1915, proposed many important and far-reaching amendments, and the constitution with these amendments, was submitted to the people on November 2, and was defeated.

In legislative bodies bills introduced often fail of enactment because they are at the time of their introduction in advance of public sentiment; but eventually they are placed upon the statute books. In constitutional conventions it likewise happens that proposals involving fundamental changes are approved by the convention, but are defeated at the polls. But, as is the case in legislative assemblies, they again make their appearance and are finally embodied in the constitution.

Honorable Joseph H. Choate was president of the convention of 1894 and Mr. Root was chairman of the Judiciary Committee and the floor leader of the majority.

Mr. Root was elected president of the New York constitutional convention of 1915. As presiding officer, he frequently took part in the general debates of the convention, regarding whose work he said in an address contained in the present volume, " We are performing the highest and most sacred duty that civilization demands from man."

The spirit in which Mr. Root approached the performance of his duties is shown by the following prayer which he made on May 5, 1915, in the absence of the chaplain:

> Almighty God, we pray to Thee to guide our deliberations this day. Make us humble, sincere, devoted to the public service. Make us wise, considerate of the feelings and the opinions and the rights of others. Make us effective and useful for the advancement of Thy cause of peace and justice and liberty in the world. For Christ's sake. Amen.

THE CONVENTION OF 1894

As the floor leader of the convention of 1894, Mr. Root made many speeches in that body, a large portion of which had to do with the procedure of the convention, while others were explanatory in their character. From the remainder, five speeches are selected, dealing with important questions and phases of government.

TRIAL BY JURY

ADDRESS OF JULY 17, 1894

The Convention having under consideration the following report from the Committee on Judiciary:

> The Committee on Judiciary, to which has been referred the proposed constitutional amendments, relating to the subject of trial by jury, respectfully reports, four members dissenting, that it has fully considered the proposed amendments, and that in the judgment of the committee no amendments should be made to the provisions of the existing constitution relating to that subject:

Mr. Root said:

I WISH to make a very few observations upon the merits of this report.

I apprehend that it is not the function of this convention to evolve a constitution out of theory or from first principles, irrespective of the existing condition of things. That is not the American or the Anglo-Saxon method of legislation. It is the French method, which has given to them within the last century many constitutions, none of which has been permanent. Our method is to proceed cautiously, slowly, holding on to that which is good, and changing only when we are certain that a change will be an improvement.

Now, sir, the fundamental idea of this report is that while there were many things which led the people of this state to order the convening of their delegates for the purpose of revising and amending the constitution, a discontent with the system of trial by jury was not one of those things. We

THE JUDICIARY

ADDRESS OF AUGUST 20, 1894

It is exceedingly difficult and yet necessary to draw the line in the Union and in the states between original and appellate jurisdiction of courts of justice. The Committee on the Judiciary of the Constitutional Convention of New York of 1894, of which Mr. Root was the chairman, dealt with this question. After much thought and reflection, the Committee presented a report, drafted by Mr. Root, drawing this distinction.

In presenting the Judiciary Article to the convention, Mr. Root made the address which follows. The whole article, consisting of twenty-three sections, was adopted by the convention practically in the form in which it was presented by Mr. Root; it was submitted to the people of the state with the remainder of the constitution at the November election of 1894, and was adopted. With certain amendments which have since been adopted, it is now a part of the organic law of the state.

IF the members of the convention will bear with me for a few minutes, I would like to explain the general scheme of reform in the judicial system of the state which is proposed by the judiciary committee. The two main evils which manifestly require treatment by this convention, so far as the judicial system is concerned, are the great delay in bringing causes to trial, in the first instance, and the great delay in securing the final disposition of causes because of the overcrowding of the calendar of the Court of Appeals. The proposed article is designed in the best way which the committee could devise to meet these two evils. So far as the first is concerned, that is to say, the overcrowding of calendars of courts of first instance, the cure is simple. It is, to bring about as great an economy of judicial force in the trial courts as possible, and to make a sufficient number of additions to those courts to enable a suitor to have his case tried at the earliest possible day. The overcrowding of calendars of trial courts exists chiefly in the great cities. It is worst in the city of the decisions of the general terms of the Supreme Court then constituted. That was so for a time, but of late years it is no longer so. Various circumstances connected with the organization and action of the general terms have brought about a state of affairs in which so large a body of appeals passes through those courts on to the Court of Appeals that that court no longer can keep up with its work and perform the function of settling and declaring the law of the state; and with this view we addressed ourselves to ascertain whether it was not possible so to constitute the intermediate appellate tribunal which we have heretofore called the general term, and so regulate the appeals from its judgments to the Court of Appeals that it would perform the function which it was originally designed to perform. We found among the reasons why the general terms are not able to stop the great body of appeals to the Court of Appeals, these: In the first place, the general term is so small, consisting of only three members, that there is not that consultation, that deliberation, that correction of one mind by another which is necessary for the satisfactory conclusions of an appellate tribunal. In the next place, as the justices of the general term are engaged in the ordinary judicial work, trying and deciding cases, and, in many instances, doing their full share of trial work, in numerous cases litigants coming before that court find that one of the judges is obliged to retire from the bench during an appeal from his own decision. And a double evil has resulted. First, that there are but two judges to pass upon the appeal — a number manifestly insufficient to secure full consultation and correction of one judgment by another. And another evil is that litigants are obliged to see the very judge from whom they are appealing going into the consultation room with the other two judges who are his associates, and upon whose decisions he is about, in the due course of the call of the calendar, to sit in review, for consultation on all the general business of the court.

And both of these have tended to decrease respect for the judgments of the general terms. Moreover, the fact that these judges in the general terms are called upon to leave that work to go to their circuits and to their special terms has led to the shortening of their hearings and to cutting down the time allowed counsel, so that counsel have been in the habit, in many places, of uniformly leaving the court feeling dissatisfied and deprived of an opportunity for the full presentation of their cases. And the judges, called away by these other duties, have been in the habit frequently of separating with their work unfinished; and we all know that it has been largely a practice for the judges of the general terms, after these brief and hurried hearings, after counsel have gone out of court dissatisfied because they have not been fully heard, to separate and, without much of any consultation, have one judge write an opinion and send it around to be concurred in, or not, as the case may be; and the tendency of all the *vis inertiæ* which exists among judges, as it does among others, has led toward concurrence rather than courting a troublesome struggle by disagreement with an opinion already written.

Then, again, the legislature has been constantly enlarging the scope of appeal from the general term to the Court of Appeals. It has opened doorway after doorway, through which constantly additional kinds of questions can be taken up to the Court of Appeals, so that the finality of the judgment of the general term has been constantly decreased, and, therefore, respect for their decisions has been decreased, and their own sense of responsibility has been decreased. Now, what we propose to do is this; we propose to divide the state into four departments, and in each department have a new appellate tribunal, which will take the place of the five general terms of the Supreme Court, and the four general terms of the Superior City Courts, nine in all, to which all appeals, from whatever tribunal, shall go in the first instance; and we propose to make that a more effective and satisfactory tribunal than the existing general terms in these ways: In the first place, by giving a greater finality to its judgments than the general terms now have; finality in a much wider range of questions, by imposing limitations upon the jurisdiction of the Court of Appeals, and on the right of appeal to that court. In the next place, by giving stability, permanence and independence to that court, through making its members hold for a fixed term; and for that purpose we provide, that they shall be selected by the governor from all the justices elected to the Supreme Court, for terms of five years; the presiding judge for a term which shall be coextensive with the remainder of his term of office in the Supreme Court. We give them also the right, the power, to govern their own sessions and to appoint their own clerk, and fix the place where his office shall be held. So that instead of being a court without a clerk, without a home, without power of self-control, shifting, variable always, its members coming in and out from the trial courts, reviewing each other's decisions, without sufficient time for the performance of their duties, it will be a real court, with power, with permanence, with stability, and worthy of the name of an appellate tribunal. We propose, further, to give an opportunity for full discussion, by making it a court of five members; and five members will have to consult. One of the presiding justices of the general term said to me some time ago, " We cannot do any more work with five judges than we can with three." " Yes," I said, " but if you have five judges, will you not consult ? " " Yes," he said, " we will." And, therefore, I say, though five judges may not do any more work than three, they will do better work and better respected work.

In the next place, we propose to give them the opportunity for deliberation, consultation and full hearing, by relieving them of the obligation of doing all other judicial work. We make it so that they cannot be called upon to sit in circuit or in special terms, or to try or determine cases. This, then, will be a real court, constituted by the conjoint action of the elective principle, through the power exercised by the people in electing justices, and the appointive principle, through the power exercised by the governor, of selection from the justices of the Supreme Court, as respectable, as able, as efficient, as any court of last resort in any state of the Union. We believe that it will be more satisfactory and effective, that its judgments will be more respected, that they will be less frequently reversed, and, therefore, less frequently appealed from than the existing general terms. Correlative to the formation of this new court, which we call the Appellate Division of the Supreme Court, is the limitation upon appeals to the Court of Appeals. In framing this we have endeavored to follow a clear line of logical distinction between the Court of Appeals and the courts of first review, a line of distinction marked out by the proper function of a court of second appeal in settling and declaring the law; and we propose to limit the Court of Appeals in two ways; first, by limiting them to the review of questions of law, and, second, by limiting appeals to them to final judgments or orders. There is a general understanding now that the proper function of a Court of Appeals is to pass only on questions of law, but there is a great class of cases which finds its way into the Court of Appeals where virtually there is a review of the question of fact for a second time, and we close the door to that class, by declaring the principle that jurisdiction shall be limited to the review of questions of law, and by providing that no unanimous decision of an appellate division that there is evidence to sustain or support a verdict not directed by the court, or a finding of fact, shall be reviewed by the Court of Appeals. So that when a man has tried his case and he has got a jury or a court to decide that a fact is proved, and five judges of the Appellate Division of the Supreme Court have unanimously held that the fact was proved, there is to be an end of controversy upon that fact. We believe that these two limitations, one limiting the court to the decision of questions of law, made effective by the supplementary provision that I have mentioned; the other limiting the review to final judgments, or orders, together with the increased respect and efficiency of the appellate division, will so greatly decrease the number of appeals to the Court of Appeals that it will for many years, will until the time comes for another constitution to be made, be able to deal with all the questions presented to it, and to keep up with its calendar. We have also, for greater certainty, and out of abundant caution, proposed the addition of two members to the bench of the Court of Appeals; and we think, or many of the committee think, that that will to some degree increase the working power of the court.

In reaching the conclusion that the course which I have outlined was the proper course to remedy the evils I have mentioned, the committee has had in contemplation several other alternatives, some of which have been proposed in amendments laid before it. And those were, first, that we might limit the jurisdiction of the Court of Appeals by fixing a moneyed amount, and preventing appeals to that court in any case which involves less than the amount fixed, following in that respect the Federal system which allows no appeal to the Supreme Court of the United States in cases involving less than five thousand dollars. But we do not believe that is a wise provision for the courts of this state. We think that as important questions of law arise in small cases as in great ones; and we believe, moreover, that the Court of Appeals of this state, the court of last resort, which is to declare the law for the guidance of all the people, ought to be all the people's court. We believe that it should be the court of the poor man, so that he may feel that he may go there if he wants to, with his question of law, as well as the court of his wealthier fellow-citizen. We believe that it is only when based upon such a foundation, that any public institution can be permanent in a free constitutional government. Therefore, instead of putting in a moneyed limit upon appeals to the Court of Appeals, we have provided that the limit now existing should be taken off, and that no such limit shall ever be imposed. Another alternative was, that we might increase the Court of Appeals so largely that it could sit in two divisions. But we might as well abolish the court and rely solely upon these four separate appellate divisions as to divide the court and have it open to the same objections which have led us to put a court above them. Another alternative was that we might do as the judiciary commission of 1890 proposed, undertake to enumerate classes of cases upon which parties might go to the Court of Appeals, leaving other classes of cases upon which they should be stopped at the tribunal of first resort. But that is uncertain, indefinite, difficult of application. It is not within human power to avoid mistakes in enumeration and definition of such classes. It may be well to attempt it when, as in the Federal Circuit Court of Appeals act, there is a statute which may be revised every year by Congress; but to undertake to place in a constitution provisions of this kind, which are certain to require amendment, is an experiment that ought to be avoided if possible. There is a substantial objection to that also that it involves an element of unfairness to the citizens who are most interested in the class of cases that are not allowed to go to the Court of Appeals; and this other objection, that the same questions of law arise in different kinds of cases; the are to wealthier men. The great body of the people of the state have only small causes. When a court is organized for the trial of small causes it ought to attend to its business and try to do it just as well as any other court tries a million-dollar cause. But, if you enlarge the jurisdiction, and give it million-dollar causes to try, it will never attend to the little causes, and you spoil your court for the trial of small causes, and merely add another court to those which try large ones. We propose by this inhibition upon the legislature, to keep a system of courts in this state which will attend to the duty of properly trying the small causes, in which the great body of the people are more interested than they are in the large ones.

SECTARIAN EDUCATION

ADDRESS OF SEPTEMBER 1, 1894

The Convention in Committee of the Whole, Mr. Charles H. Truax in the chair, having under consideration a report relative to the use of public moneys for sectarian education, Mr. Root said:

I CAME to this convention, Mr. Chairman, in common with many of my fellow-delegates, expecting to vote to prohibit all state aid to any sectarian institution, whether educational or charitable. It is with regret that I have found an impression gaining ground in the convention that the attempt to prohibit such aid to sectarian charitable institutions might better be abandoned, and that a proposition made by the advocates of such aid might better be accepted, to the effect that there should be merely supervision of aid to charitable institutions, and not absolute prohibition. I now find, sir, that the very gentlemen who have been seeking to secure the acquiescence of this convention in leaving charitable institutions free from a prohibition, are insisting upon attaching to the proposition against state aid to sectarian institutions a proviso, which, in my judgment, if adopted, will send us out of this convention, not merely having failed to prohibit state aid to sectarian education, but having absolutely put into the constitution an authorization of such aid. There can be no mistake, Mr. Chairman, about the effect of the proviso offered by Mr. Lauterbach, from New York; no mistake as to effect of the proviso offered by Mr. Marshall, from Onondaga. They both mean, and both accomplish, so far as the subject I am now discussing is concerned, the same thing. After the clear and emphatic declaration contained in section four of the proposed article, that the money of the state shall not be used in aid or maintenance of any school or institution of learning wholly or in part under the control or direction of any religious denomination, or in which any denominational tenet is taught, it is now proposed to say that this section shall not prohibit the appropriation of money for secular instruction, to the inmates of any orphan asylum or of any institution to which children may be committed by judicial process, if such education is incidental only; and that is, by the most friendly rules of construction, equivalent to putting into this proposition these words: " We hereby authorize the use of public money for the maintenance of charitable institutions under sectarian control and for instruction in schools connected therewith, under sectarian and denominational control." That, sir, is the act we are now invited to substitute for the contemplated prohibition of all state aid to sectarian charities.

I, for one, sir, will never vote for an article which contains such a constitutional authorization of state aid to sectarian institutions, or for any constitution which contains such an article; and I believe, sir, that the great body of the people of this state will refuse to give their sanction to any such provision. It is unnecessary, sir, to accomplish the purposes of the gentlemen who offer it; for there is not a man in this convention who has suggested or will suggest that the section, as it now stands, in the slightest degree interferes with the use of the state money for the maintenance of any orphan asylum, or any house of refuge, or any charitable institution; or in the slightest degree interferes with the use of the money of the state for the support or maintenance of any inmate of any charitable institution, even though that institution may be under sectarian control, and even though instruction may be given in it. The proviso proposed can do nothing to accomplish any benefit for the institutions in which these gentlemen are interested, but it throws open the doors for the accomplishment of what we all of us here have agreed to avoid, the giving of state aid to sectarian instruction.

The gentleman from Jefferson calls it a small thing. I beg leave to say, sir, that it is the greatest question and most important principle which has come before this convention, or will come before it until its final adjournment. Your fathers, Mr. Chairman, came to this country from that heroic little land in which Spanish soldiers under the iron hand of Philip the Second and the Duke of Alva strove to impress the power of the State of Spain upon the consciences of William the Silent and John of Barneveldt. Mine left their English homes in the reign of Charles the First, to escape that controlling force of Church and State united, which forbade them liberty of conscience. They came to a barbarous and inhospitable shore; they fought and conquered the savage; they felled the forests; they cleared the land; they established a state; they secured their independence of foreign control. They set up a reign of law and order, of peace and prosperity; and then they opened their hands of welcome to the fathers of the gentlemen who propose this amendment; they opened their hands to the fathers of the gentleman from New York, to the fathers of the gentleman from Onondaga, to the fathers of the gentlemen upon the other side of the chamber, who are so anxious to have this proviso inserted; and they welcomed them, not to savage and inhospitable shores, not to wars with savage foes, not to privation and hardship, but to a peaceful and a happy land, where home and comfort met them at the threshold, and they gave to them the freest exercise of conscience; they welcomed their religions with them, forgetful of all the tyranny they themselves had endured; they welcomed Hebrew and Catholic alike; they imposed no hostile, or professional, or business, or social bar against the full exercise of religion and the full privilege of citizenship, upon religious ground; but, Mr. Chairman, there is one thing, and one thing only, which this people, generous, broadminded, and liberal, said, have always said, and say today, that never in this state of ours shall be repeated that union of Church and State, which drove your fathers and mine from their homes in the old world. And that, sir, is the principle which we seek to embody in this constitution of ours by the declaration reported by the Committee on Education. It is the greatest principle which this convention has opportunity to declare. And, Mr. Chairman, it should be, it must be, it shall be, cut down, modified, affected by no proviso, by no limitation, to secure or protect any private interest. Therefore, I believe that every true American, of whatever religion, will be for this section as it stands now. It is not a question of religion, or of creed, or of party; it is a question of declaring and maintaining the great American principle of eternal separation between Church and State.

THE POLITICAL USE OF MONEY

ADDRESS OF SEPTEMBER 3, 1894

It is recognized in democracies, where public officers are elected and questions of government are passed upon by the people, that political campaigns become in a large measure educational campaigns, and that for this purpose considerable sums of money can legitimately and wisely be expended. At the same time, there is a tendency on the part of unscrupulous politicians to make an improper use of money. The difficulty is to draw the line of demarkation between the legitimate and the corrupt use of money in political campaigns, and by apt laws to proscribe the illegitimate use of money and by criminal proceedings to punish both violators and violations of the law.

In the constitutional convention of 1894, the following amendments were proposed to article 2 of the constitution:

Section 6. The legislature shall, by general laws, declare the uses which may be lawfully made of money or other valuable things by, or on behalf of, any person, to promote his nomination as a candidate for public office, and by or on behalf of a candidate to promote his election.

The use or promise of money or other valuable thing to promote the nomination for, or election to, public office of any person otherwise than is expressly authorized by law, is prohibited and the person by whom or for whose benefit, with his consent, connivance or procurement the same is so used or promised, if elected, shall forfeit his office.

Section 7. No corporation shall directly or indirectly use any of its money or property for, or in aid of, any political party or organization, or for, or in aid of, any candidate for political office or for nomination for such office, or in any manner use any of its money or property for any political purpose whatever, or for the reimbursement or indemnification of any person for moneys or property so used.

Every domestic corporation which violates this section shall forfeit its charter, and every foreign corporation which violates this section shall forfeit the right to do business in this state.

Both sections, as above, were adopted in the Committee of the Whole, but neither section was incorporated in the final draft of the constitution.

It is interesting to note that New York seems to have been the first state to enact laws against corrupt practices at elections. In 1890 the legislature passed a law requiring candidates to file an itemized statement of expenditures on penalty of imprisonment and loss of the office. In 1909, the legislature passed a law substantially in the words of the proposed amendment of 1894, prohibiting corporations, except political associations, from contributing to campaign funds or for any political purposes whatsoever.

While the two amendments above quoted were under consideration in the Committee of the Whole, on September 3, 1894, Mr. Root made the following addresses:

THE object of this provision, Mr. Chairman, is to lay down a general principle, to which the laws of the state shall conform, which is in accordance with what I believe to be the most enlightened sentiment of the time, and to fix the expressions of that sentiment in the constitution; to require the legislature in its laws to conform to it, and require the legislature to say what money may be used to procure the election of a candidate. Until that is done, there is absolutely no limit to corruption, no limit to the purchase of votes, no limit to the improper influence of voters, or of parties, or of party men. And you perceive that putting the two paragraphs in section 6 together, there is an entirely different state of affairs produced from that which now exists. By the first paragraph the legislature is required to declare affirmatively what uses of money may lawfully be made. That is a very different thing from prohibition. It is required to declare affirmatively, to enumerate the uses which may be made; and by the second paragraph all other uses than those expressly authorized are prohibited, and are made a ground for forfeiture of office. That is a very small step in the direction of the Corrupt Practices Act in force in England, which has worked such admirable results in respect of the election of the members of Parliament. Just so long as you undertake to enumerate your prohibitions upon the use of money, just so long evasions of those prohibitions will always be possible. But, if you enumerate the ways in which money may be used, affirmatively enumerate them, and then confine candidates for office, party committees, party agents, the agents of candidates, — confine them to those uses, and as a penalty for any knowing departure from those limitations, forfeiture of the office, you will have a very different state of affairs in respect to what we will all agree, I am sure, has become one of the great and crying evils of our politics; the enormous use of money in all our elections.

The use of money has come to such a pass at the hands of both of the great political parties in this country that we find enormous contributions necessary to maintain party machinery, to conduct party warfare; and the effect is that great moneyed interests, corporate and personal, are exerting yearly more and more undue influence in political affairs. Great moneyed interests are becoming more and more necessary to the support of political parties, and political parties are every year contracting greater debts to the men who can furnish the money to perform the necessary functions of party warfare. The object of this amendment is, by laying down a simple rule, to put an end, if possible, to that great crying evil of American politics. It may not accomplish everything, it may not be sufficient to end the evil wholly, but it is a step in the right direction, and is of a character which it is proper to incorporate in the constitution.

POLITICAL CONTRIBUTIONS BY CORPORATIONS

On the same date, Mr. Root spoke as follows on the proposed section 7, prohibiting political contributions by corporations:

THE idea of section 7, Mr. Chairman, is to prevent the great moneyed corporations of the country from furnishing the money with which to elect members of the legislature of this state, in order that those members of the legislature may vote to protect the corporations. It is to prevent the great railroad companies, the great insurance companies, the great telephone companies, the great aggregations of wealth, from using their corporate funds, directly or indirectly, to send members of the legislature to these halls, in order to vote for their protection and the advancement of their interests as against those of the public.

It strikes, Mr. Chairman, at a constantly growing evil in our political affairs, which has, in my judgment, done more to shake the confidence of the plain people of small means in our political institutions, than any other practice which has ever obtained since the foundation of our government. And I believe that the time has come when something ought to be done to put a check upon the giving of $50,000 or $100,000 by a great corporation toward political purposes, upon the understanding that a debt is created from a political party to it; a debt to be recognized and repaid with the votes of representatives in the legislature and in Congress, or by the action of administrative or executive officers who have been elected in a measure through the use of the money so contributed.

It is precisely because laws aimed directly at the crime of bribery so far have been ineffective, that we deem it advisable to provide limitations short of the actual commission of the crime. I apprehend that many political committees and many candidates for office, if not most political committees and most candidates for office, will refuse to sanction a use of money which is prohibited in so solemn a manner, even though the prohibition be not affixed simply to a crime, and that that limitation being upon matters which are not done in the dark, but which are necessarily open and public to a great extent, would be much more easily enforced than the prohibition against the crime of bribery directly. I apprehend that many corporations, which are now called upon before every election to contribute large sums of money to campaign funds, would find in an absolute prohibition, with the penalty of the forfeiture of their charters, a reason why they would not make such contributions. I think it will be a protection to corporations and to candidates against demands upon them, and a protection to the people against the payment of consideration for contributions by them, to the injury of the representation of the people. It is, I repeat, because of the difficulty of proving and punishing the crime of buying votes, that some other measures seem to be desirable.

THE CIVIL SERVICE

ADDRESS OF SEPTEMBER 21, 1894

The following amendment to the constitution was adopted as section 9 of article V:

> Section 9. Appointments and promotions in the civil service of the state, and of all the civil divisions thereof, including cities and villages, shall be made according to merit and fitness, to be ascertained, so far as practicable, by examinations, which, so far as practicable, shall be competitive; provided, however, that honorably discharged soldiers and sailors from the army and navy of the United States in the late Civil War, who are citizens and residents of this state, shall be entitled to preference in appointment and promotion without regard to their standing on any list from which such appointment or promotion may be made. Laws shall be made to provide for the enforcement of this section.

While this amendment was under consideration in Committee of the Whole, Mr. Root spoke as follows:

I WISH to explain my vote. I am in favor of this amendment because I believe it puts into the constitution a principle, one of the most salutary of recent advancements in government. I believe in regard to that principle just what President Grant believed when, in his message to Congress in 1870, he recommended a provision for civil service reform, and said of civil service: "I would have it govern not the tenure but the manner of making all appointments." And said further: "The present system does not secure the best men and not even fit men for public office." I am not willing to stand, and I should regret to see my associates stand, upon any lower ground than that best and warmest of friends occupied twenty-four years ago. I believe, sir, that this principle ought to be incorporated in the constitution because it is right, and because I do not regard the words of party platforms as being mere buncombe, to be disregarded at will. Whatever may be the practice of the gentlemen who have been amusing themselves by sneers today upon the other side of the chamber as to regard for their party platform, I believe, sir, in the civil service plank of the platforms to which I have given my adherence in years past, and shall vote accordingly today.

I think, sir, we should adopt this amendment for another and practical reason. As the matter stands today, the court of last resort has ruled that the principle of civil service cannot be applied to the important positions in the State Prisons and Public Works Department, and the effect of this amendment will be to extend this reform to state prisons and canals; and it will complete the adoption by this convention of the recommendations of the Prison Commission, which were that by constitutional amendment the system of contract labor should be abolished and the state prisons be taken out of politics. For these reasons, Mr. President, I am for the amendment as it stands, and I vote aye.

THE CONVENTION OF 1915

THE PRINCIPLES AND PRACTICE OF CONSTITUTIONAL REVISION

ADDRESS AS PRESIDING OFFICER AT THE DINNER MEETING OF THE ACADEMY OF POLITICAL SCIENCE, NEW YORK CITY
NOVEMBER 19, 1914

THERE is an interesting parallel between the present constitutional convention and the one that preceded it. The last one ought to have occurred in 1887, twenty years after the convention of 1867. It did not please the party which happened to be in power in 1887 and for a number of years afterward to have the convention, because they could not get the arrangements just to suit them. At last, in 1892, everything was right and the convention was brought on; delegates were elected in 1893, and a convention was held in 1894. But, lo, after everything was right and the convention was determined upon, there came a revolution in the politics of the state, and the other party elected a majority of delegates and controlled the convention.

At this time it seemed to some one — I do not know to whom — that it would be a bright stroke of politics to advance the convention, and so a special election was held, and the convention was brought on by a narrow majority, composed in part, we already know through judicial decisions, of fraudulent votes. But lo, after the convention was thus determined upon, a revolution occurred and the other party controls the convention.

And the lesson is that it does not pay to be too acute and adroit and cunning in American politics. The best way is to go on in a simple, direct, honest, faithful effort to help the working of our free self-government. Whoever does that will go ahead of the very smart politicians every time.

I wish to mention another parallel, or contrast, between the two conventions which I think is cause for great satisfaction. In September, 1894, the convention of that year had substantially completed its work, and had taken a recess for a few days to enable the committee on revision to give the last careful consideration to the terms or form of the work. I went up from Albany to Saratoga, where the Republican convention was held. I found myself put upon the committee on resolutions; I attended the meeting of the committee, and some one produced a platform which had been prepared and which was handed to the chairman of the committee. The platform was read, or run through hastily, and the chairman was about to put it to a vote. I noticed that no mention was made in this platform of the work of the constitutional convention — a convention the majority of which was composed of Republicans, nominated and elected by Republican votes. We thought that the convention had done some good things; but it was not considered of sufficient consequence to mention in the resolutions of the Republican convention which met immediately after the work was completed. I made some observations upon that subject, and was very loyally seconded by a gentleman for whom I have always had the kindliest feeling, the late Timothy L. Woodruff, and a clause was put into the platform approving the work of the convention. This year I went to Saratoga to attend the Republican convention, and there were present between twenty and thirty of the ablest leaders of opinion from all parts of the state of New York, who spent three days in discussing the question as to what position the Republican party ought to take in regard to the work of the constitutional convention. That marks a change in the public attitude towards questions of government.

And this meeting is something which twenty years ago never had a parallel. The members of that convention evolved out of their inner consciousness the provisions which seemed to them to be good for the state; and they had little help from anybody except the people who had a particular ax to grind. I don't care much whether people when they start are thinking right or wrong; I don't feel any apprehension about the people being too radical, or being too conservative. So long as the thoughtful people of the Republic will take a real interest in questions of government, will think about them and discuss them, so long we are sure to come out right.

Twenty years ago the thought and the feelings of the people of this state were asleep on fundamental questions of government. Today the thoughts and the feelings of the people of this state are awake, and interest is keen. Consequently I feel the greatest confidence in the product — not so much in the deliberations of the convention itself, as in the force of the intelligent, instructed, and mature public opinion of the state, operating upon the minds of the members of that convention.

Now let me say something practical about your work for the convention. The time is rapidly passing during which abstract discussion can be made useful. The convention will meet in the first week in April, and when that time comes it will be too late for the processes of general instruction. All the discussion that has been going on during these recent years, the discussion you are having now, must be brought into converging lines of practical suggestions — definite, certain, positive, practical suggestions, not discussions of theories of government, but helpful proposals as to what shall be written into the constitution.

The convention meets, I say, the first week in April. The time during which any suggestions can be made after the meeting begins will be very short, because we soon run into sometimes a young man who begins life with brilliant talents, undertakes this profession, and presently, finding it difficult, turns to another, and after a while leaves that and turns to another, and then to still another. His life is wasted. There is a little tendency of that kind in government. No great principle can be applied year after year, and generation after generation, where the people develop incompetency, and cease to grow in intelligent capacity. No principle can be applied without meeting obstacles, and being surrounded by inconveniences, and having the faint-hearted say, " Let us find some other way to work out our salvation. Oh, to abandon the hard and painful and trying effort!"

To grow in power, to grow in capacity for true liberty and true justice by holding fast to true principles, is hard. There are many who grow tired, who would find some easier way; but the easier way will but lead from the true path into some other easy way, and that into some other. Self-government, which is the basis and essence of our free republican government, is hard and discouraging. It requires courage and persistency and true patriotism to keep the grip on the handle of the plow and drive the furrow through. But wherever there is a true principle embodied in our constitution, we must stand by it and maintain it against all patent nostrums.

On the other hand, there are indications extensive and numerous of a reaction from certain extreme views, from certain enthusiasm for new devices in government. But we must remember that if reaction goes too far the pendulum will swing back the other way. All our statements of principle must be re-examined, not with faint hearts, but with a sincere purpose to ascertain whether the statement is sound and right, and whether it needs modification with reference to the new conditions in order more perfectly to express the principle.

I feel very differently about this convention from the way in which I felt twenty years ago, because it seems to me that upon this field of action dealing with the fundamental principles of our government we are performing the highest and most sacred duty that civilization ever demands from man. All the little questions of form and method may be right or wrong; we may solve them rightly or wrongly. If they are wrong they will be changed. If the law is wrong it will be changed. If it is not perfect it will be amended. But when a people undertakes to state fundamental principles of its government, it is putting to the test its right and its power to live. Millions of men in western Europe today who are battling with each other, dying by the thousands, are fighting upon one side or the other of two different conceptions of national morality. Homes are desolated, children left fatherless, because two great principles of national morality have met in their death-grip. The nation which lays hold of the truth, of the true principles of liberty and justice will live. The nation that is wrong, the nation that fails to grasp the truth, will die. In our effort or attempt to make and remake the constitutions of our beloved country we are putting to the test the very life of the country. To that task we should address ourselves with the prayer that we may be free from selfishness. That task should be performed with a sense of duty to one's country that rises to the level of religion. With the help of all the good men and women of our state we should be able to keep this convention right, upon the eternal principles by which alone our free and peaceful and just country can continue.

I thank you, gentlemen, for this greeting and for the great compliment of your gathering here at a luncheon which is avowedly for the purpose of making me the guest of the Association. There is but one disadvantage in the vastness of this assemblage, and that is that it is necessary in talking with you to talk very loud, and it is quite impossible for any one, in loud tones of voice, to be quite as sensible as he can sometimes be in ordinary conversation. There is always a temptation to attempt oratory, and as a rule oratory and sense are to be found in inverse proportions.

There is a substantial satisfaction to me, not all personal, in this great gathering; it is a satisfaction due to perceiving that the business men of New York are at last taking an interest in their own public affairs; that you are at last taking an interest in the over-head charges of all your business, which are created by the conduct of government; that you are at last taking an interest, before it is too late, in the law and the administration which create opportunity or hamper enterprise. Do not think that I am dropping into oratory when I say that. There are great parts of the people of the United States who feel that the man who makes any money by successful business is a robber, and it is time that that feeling was dispelled and that that view should become a vagary of the past.

Now, Americans must always keep their faces toward the future, and the thing that is admittedly before us in a public way in this state is the revision of the state constitution. There are a few things I want to say to you about that.

In the first place, I bespeak your interest for the work of the constitutional convention. It needs speaking for. The votes in this state upon questions of constitutional amendment have ordinarily been most pitiful in number; only from a quarter to a half of the people voting at our elections have taken interest enough to cast votes for or against amendments of the constitution. It seems sometimes as if our people were interested in nothing but personalities, and that we wanted a government of men and not a government of laws. It seems sometimes as if our people do not realize that it makes any difference to them what laws they have or how they are administered. I am glad to see that there is a change in that opinion. I beg you to follow with interest the work of this convention and to take sufficient interest in it to consider and discuss and vote upon the results.

Let me tell you that it is none too soon for you to be interested. The business man of America has been at a heavy discount of recent years. All other elements of our population have organized and been active in their own behalf. The agriculturalists have organized and their representatives have been heard from. The labor men have been organized and their representatives can be seen day by day in the galleries of the two Houses of Congress, watching the men who are making the laws to see whether they shall win the great prize of the labor vote or lose it by independence.

The business man alone has seemed to be paralyzed of recent years, and the delightful thing about this meeting is that this is something besides paper organization. There are plenty of concerns on paper — there are plenty of men going about and talking about the great interests they represent — and they don't represent anybody but themselves. But here is evidence that the men who are represented are really behind their representatives — that there is something besides paper organization, something besides oratory stirring in the interests of the great industry and commerce and production of the United States. And if you will follow the line that you have entered upon it will soon come to be no longer true that the pursuit of profitable business is to be regarded as robbery. For after all it is you, it is the voters of New York, who must pass upon a revision of the constitution. When the work is done and submitted you must vote for it or against it; you must act upon it ignorantly or advisedly, and if you do not take interest enough to be informed and to inform your neighbors about the merits of it, it will go by default.

A second thing I want to say is: Do not expect the convention to do too much. It ought not to do too much; it had better do too little than too much. It is not the office of the convention to turn everything upside down and to sweep all our system away and inaugurate a new one. Our laws, fundamental and ordinary, are to be based upon our history. It is not the function of legislators in Congress or legislature, or constitutional convention to put into a law what happens to occur to them as being a pretty good thing. It is their function faithfully to register the customs and mature conclusions of the people whom they serve, so that each successive step in legislative development may be but a record of the growth and development of our life.

We are attracted from day to day by new schemes of reform, many of them most praiseworthy, many of them most necessary. Today we are interested in this one, and tomorrow in another and the next day in a third. But after all, the all-important thing is the preservation of the great body of the rights and liberties of our self-governing people which have been growing year by year, century by century, since Magna Charta, and under which we live now in peace and order and opportunity for posterity and for growth in spirit and in power.

It will be the first and greatest duty of the convention which is about to meet to preserve all that is good, all that has been approved of, all that has been tried in our system of free self-government. I would rather see a legislature praised for doing little and doing it well than see it praised for doing much. A very wise old friend of mine said, many years ago, "It does not make so much difference how much a man does as what he does."

We are seeing now in the newspapers remarks that this legislature has not done much. I had a count made not long ago in the Library of Congress of the number of laws that had been passed in the five preceding years. That was made last year, and in the five years ended the first of December, 1913, I found that over sixty-two thousand laws had been passed by Congress and the state legislatures in this country in that five years; and I found that there had been reported during that five years and published in six hundred and thirty volumes of reports of the courts over sixty-five thousand decisions of courts of last resort in this country. Now even Mr. Choate does not know them all by heart. How can you possibly know them ? How can you conduct your business and keep out of jail ? So, give credit to the convention for what it does not do.

A third thing is: Do not be out of patience with us if we discuss at wearisome length the proposals that are brought before the convention. Remember that long discussion, free, open, unrestrained and unchecked discussion in representative assemblies under our form of representative government, is the substitute for war. In Mexico today you see the other method of conducting government. You must have, among a virile people, differences of opinion, with men adhering to their opinion with determination; and there are only two ways to reach the conclusions that are necessary for peace and honor. One is the way of discussing them, arguing them out, getting to conclusions by long and painful discussion, and the other is by shooting the man that is opposed to you. Our system is the first, so when we talk for long days in the heat of summer over the questions we have before us, remember that we are a great Peace Society.

But there is one thing which the convention, I feel, ought to do. The business of government in this state, and in most of our states, has outgrown the machinery; or many of our states, I will say, have outgrown the machinery of government. Our machinery, executive and legislative and judicial, was established in simpler times; it was established when government interfered much less in the affairs of the people than it is compelled to do now. The change from individualism, from individual activity to combined activity, has made it necessary for government to do many things which were formerly left to the individual.

We are all dependent upon each other; we are all interdependent. The great combinations of capital and of labor; the dependence of each man, in his ordinary life, upon the activities — the continued activities — of a multitude of other men, for his breakfast, his light, his heat, his access to the street, the preservation of his health or that of his family, for education, for transportation, all make it necessary that there should be government regulation of the activities of life. Now in these later days of complicated government activity affecting the vast multitude of interests, of occupations and of social relations in our state, the time clearly has come when the machinery of government shall be reformed so that it shall be competent to attend to the business. We are running a railroad with a stage-coach organization.

We should learn a lesson from those great business organizations which have reduced the price of production and enlarged the boundaries of commerce, and have made the production of wealth in these recent years the subject of the astonishment of mankind. We should learn a lesson from business, from business men, from the great business geniuses of our country, and apply that lesson to the affairs of our government.

The first thing — the one all-important thing — is to make the organization so that responsibility shall be fixed. You and I don't know who is really responsible in our state government for what goes wrong or for what goes right. We don't know who really are to be blamed, and we don't know who really ought to be praised; and there is no way of having effective service in government any more than in a business enterprise unless you can put your finger on the man who is responsible for this error, or should be commended for that success.

And in order that there shall be responsibility, power must go with the responsibility. You cannot hold men responsible unless you give them power. The Governor of the state to-day is being unjustly criticised for not doing things that our system withholds the power to do from him, and that will be so until we have improved the system on business principles.

When that has been done, we can hold somebody accountable. But, gentlemen, the doing of it is going to meet with obstacles. The doing of it is going to turn some people out of office — is going to withdraw from some people the opportunities for office which they have been looking forward to. Individual interests and local interests and special corporate interests are going to feel themselves interfered with. It often happens, when public interest has not been aroused, that it seems in the course of government as if the only consideration that had no friends was the consideration that rested only upon the public good. It is for you, with your practical business sense, to put yourselves behind whatever the convention may find it practicable to do for the promotion of the public interests, and to give it the force and momentum of your support as against all private and local individual interests and prejudices; and I can assure you that this gathering of the business men of New York will give greater life and hope and courage to the members of the coming constitutional convention who are sitting about me at this table. One thing we shall miss, and that is the noble and courageous and brilliant leadership of the man who presided over the deliberations of the last convention.

We shall miss him sadly, but, Heaven be praised, his spirit and the benign influence of his character and the inspiration of his genius will still be with us, and we shall do all that we can fairly be called upon to do — our best — for the interests of our beloved state and our beloved country.

OPENING ADDRESS

AS PRESIDENT OF THE CONSTITUTIONAL CONVENTION
STATE OF NEW YORK, APRIL 6, 1915

The delegates to the constitutional convention of 1915 were elected, sixteen at large and three from each of the fifty-one senatorial districts of the state, making a total membership of 169.

The convention met in the assembly chamber in the Capitol at Albany on April 6, 1915, and proceeded to elect Mr. Root its president by a vote of 129 to 32 for Mr. Morgan J. O'Brien. The election was immediately made unanimous and thereupon Mr. Root delivered the following address:

I THANK you for the great honor that you have conferred in making me your president. I prize very highly the confidence which it implies. The presiding officer of the convention can accomplish nothing of value without your unselfish support, but I feel sure of having that, and with it I shall try to administer fairly the rules of parliamentary law which are based upon the experience derived through centuries of growth in representative government. Observance of such rules is indispensable to the free, open, public discussion in representative assemblies essential to the conduct of popular government. Upon the real freedom and sincerity of our discussions and the evidences of matured judgment which we present in assigning the reasons for our conclusions will depend to a great degree the approval or rejection of our labors; for the people themselves will pass upon our work in the light of the reasons we present and our revision will receive its effect by their vote and not by ours.

The most obvious duty before us is to scrutinize attentively the framework of the state government in order to ascertain in what respect, if any, the established institutions are insufficient or ill-adapted to accomplish the ends of government. Great changes have come in the industrial and social life of the state since the last convention. To attain the ends which every one agrees ought to be attained it appears necessary that government shall interfere to a much greater extent than in former times with the complicated and interdependent life of the people. The business which government is required to undertake has vastly increased both in magnitude and variety and there is a widespread feeling that in some respects the business of the government has outgrown the organization of government. Many thoughtful citizens consider that our system of taxation, appropriation, and expenditure of moneys, which worked very well in simpler times, is now quite inadequate. Many think that the strictly municipal interests of our great cities require more protection in the way of home rule provisions than is afforded in the present constitution. Many think that the natural resources of the state, particularly the forests and water power, should be brought under a system of conservation and utilization having the stability of a constitutional basis.

Many think that our ballot has become too complicated and unwieldy and that the real power of the voter over the affairs of government would be increased if there were fewer candidates to be voted for, and fewer subjects for the voter to pass upon, at the same time. Many think that the great multitude of separate offices and commissions which have been created from time to time to meet new demands for official action should be brought into more definite relations with each other and under more systematic supervision and control.

These and other subjects have enlisted the interest of respectable bodies of citizens who are entitled to have from this convention attentive consideration of their opinions. I will not continue the enumeration or enter upon a discussion of the subjects to be presented further than to say that we have before us in our own country signal examples of great business organizations for production and commerce, through which conservation of resources, economy of expenditure, and effectiveness of action have been attained to a very high degree, and citizens concerned in the great business of government may well learn a lesson from these examples.

The fundamental principle to be applied I take to be that responsibility and power shall always go together. Responsibility without power can never be justly enforced, and power without responsibility can never be duly controlled. Vague, indefinite, uncertain, overlapping, and conflicting grants of power and divided responsibility make good administration impossible. Every public officer and agent should have clear and definite authority to do the acts required of him and should have some one over him with authority to hold him to responsibility, from the lowest employee to the highest elected officer whom the people themselves hold to responsibility at the polls. Grants of power should be clear and definite, and the responsibility should be open, public, ascertained, and unmistakable, so that praise and blame, reward and punishment, may be assigned by the people themselves with justice and certainty.

In all our labors let us keep in mind that it is our duty, so far as our powers go, to preserve as well as to improve. While we seek to adapt the machinery of government to changing conditions, we are still to preserve the great body of rights and liberties which have grown through many centuries of political and juridical development, and under which we have so long been blessed by peace, order, justice, and individual liberty and opportunity. It is not for us to tear down institutions based upon the customs and growing out of the life of the people whom we serve, merely for the purpose of substituting in their place creations of our own devising, however confident we may feel in the success of the experiments we may contemplate.

the individual will is limited only by the equal rights of all other individuals. The rights of the individual citizen to life, to liberty, to the pursuit of happiness, are held by indefeasible title. He cannot rightfully be deprived of those rights by legislatures or executives or majorities or armies. To secure the equal rights of every one of the ten million people of the state of New York is the end and object of all that we are to do; and an affirmation of the sacredness of those equal and inalienable individual rights, is the primary maxim of the political morality which is to direct our conduct.

This is the seventh of the conventions meeting in orderly succession during the one hundred and thirty-nine years which have elapsed since New York was a colony. One who reviews the labors of the men that strove with the problems of their day in 1777, in 1801, in 1821, in 1846, in 1867, and in 1894 cannot fail to be impressed by the evidence that the problems of government never end. Settled for the moment they continually reappear in slightly varying forms upon the requirement of new conditions. Yet the unending effort for solution is the process which gives direction to the development of national life.

Above all our predecessors we are fortunate in serving a community itself inspired by an unprecedented interest in the subjects with which we are to deal, appreciating their importance, eager in discussion, fruitful of suggestion, desirous to contribute to a wise conclusion. That condition is a cheerful harbinger of the future, for indifference is the deadliest foe of democracy. A people alive to its problems is certain to move forward. If by thorough study and practical sense and sincerity of purpose we can lead this great discussion among the self-governing people of the state, even though not a line we write were voted into the constitution, this convention will not have failed in its purpose of usefulness to its generation.

MAGNA CHARTA

ADDRESS BEFORE THE CONSTITUTIONAL CONVENTION IN COMMEMORATION OF THE SEVEN HUNDREDTH ANNIVERSARY OF MAGNA CHARTA, JUNE 15, 1915

THE convention appointed by the people of the state to revise the fundamental law under which we live, as to the framework of government and the principles of public morality, has deemed it appropriate to arrange for a celebration of the seven hundredth anniversary of the signing of Magna Charta.

That was a great event in English history. The restrained and unemotional English themselves, in their most formal public documents, describe it as the Great Charter of English liberty. But it is not merely as a great event in English history that we celebrate it. It was a great event in our history, and it was a great event in the world's history.

That instrument which the barons compelled King John to sign contained no rhetoric; it did not philosophize; it was a plain, practical assertion of common rights fitted to the use of the people of England of that day. Hundreds of great declarations of principles have been made and forgotten since that time, but this simple, homely growth from the life of the English people has endured these seven hundred years.

The Charter was not a gift of privilege by the monarch. Hundreds of monarchs have granted privileges to their subjects since that time and the privileges have been forgotten, and the monarchs with them. It was an assertion of right by men who were willing to fight for their rights, and to die for them. And during all these seven hundred years, the men to whom that has been the Great Charter of liberties have been willing to fight for their liberties and to die for them.

But even those qualities were not the essential thing which kept alive this wonderful instrument, for seven hundred years. The essential thing was that the Great Charter asserted a principle of human liberty upon which rests the development of the freedom of the world. It asserted — it did not ask for — it asserted the rights of Englishmen as against their government, and superior to their government. Without rhetoric, without reasoning, without philosophy, it asserted those rights which, nearly six hundred years later, the sons of those Englishmen crystallized in the Declaration of American Independence, as the inalienable rights of man, to secure which governments are created.

There are but two underlying theories of man in the social relation to the state: One is the theory of the ancient republics, under which the state is the starting point from which rights are deduced, and the individual holds rights only as a member of the state. That was the theory of Greece, and Rome, and the Italian republics. The other is the theory of the Great Charter, the theory of the Habeas Corpus Act, of the Statute of Treasons, of the Petition of Rights, of the Bill of Rights, of the Massachusetts Body of Liberties, of the Declaration of Independence, of the American Republic, that the individual has inalienable rights, of which no government may deprive him, but to secure which all government exists.

The first theory, of the ancient republic, that the state is all in all and the individual derives his rights as a member, leads to the logical and inevitable result that the state is free from those rules of morality by which individual men are bound. It is the principle which was applied in Belgium. It is the principle which was applied to the *Lusitania.*

The other, asserted in the Great Charter, by logical and inevitable result binds the state by the rules of morality which the individual recognizes; and this supremacy of that rule of right, governing all men and all states and powers, is the hope of mankind.

The assertion of that great and eternal principle seven hundred years ago we celebrate as the greatest of all events in the political development of modern liberty.

IMPEACHMENT

ADDRESS BEFORE THE CONSTITUTIONAL CONVENTION
AUGUST 20, 1915

The constitutional convention of 1915 proposed to amend article VIII, section 15, of the constitution of 1894, so that it would read as follows, the amendment being indicated in italics:

> Section 15. The assembly shall have the power of impeachment, by a vote of a majority of all the members elected. The court for the trial of impeachments shall be composed of the president of the senate, the senators, or the major part of them, and the judges of the court of appeals, or the major part of them. *On the trial of an impeachment against the governor or lieutenant-governor, neither the lieutenant-governor nor the president of the senate shall act as a member of the court. The court for the trial of impeachments may order all or any part of the testimony to be taken and reported by a committee composed of members of the court, except that the impeached officer must be allowed to testify before the court if he so desire.* No judicial officer shall exercise his office, after articles of impeachment against him shall have been preferred to the senate, until he shall have been acquitted. Before the trial of an impeachment the members of the court shall take an oath or affirmation truly and impartially to try the impeachment according to the evidence, and no person shall be convicted without the concurrence of two-thirds of the members present. Judgment in cases of impeachment shall not extend further than to removal from office, or removal from office and disqualification to hold and enjoy any office of honor, trust or profit under this state; but the party impeached shall be liable to indictment and punishment according to law.

When this article, as amended, was before the Committee of the Whole, Mr. Root made the following remarks:

AN impeachment is not a criminal proceeding. The express provision of our constitution, the common provision of constitutions, is that judgment shall not extend beyond removal from office to which disqualification from future holding of office may be added and the party impeached may still be indictable and punished, according to law.

These very precise and rigid rules of protection of defendants in criminal cases, are out of tenderness of the law for liberty and life, which are not called in question at all in impeachment cases. An impeachment is purely a matter between the people and their political agent, and the great obstacle to the successful use of impeachment as a means of enabling the people to deal with their unfaithful servants arises from the fact that an impeachment stops the wheels of government. The injury to the conduct of the affairs of government is so great that it does not pay to impeach unless there is a very, very serious case and a scandal which leads the public to demand that there shall be action. And there ought to have been more than four impeachments in this state, and a great many more. We would have had a better government and a more contented people if this remedy had been more practical and available so that more unfaithful officers should have been called to account.

The inadequacy of the remedy has been such that over a large part of our country people have been demanding — what? Not that public officials should have their office secured by the right of trial before a court and impartial tribunal, with the right to be confronted with the witnesses, with the right to specific charges, with the right to require that the charges be affirmatively proven, with the right of judicial judgment upon the proof, but that they should be liable to be recalled by a popular vote cast upon the information obtained from the columns of the newspapers. I say it is the inadequacy of the remedy of impeachment which has led to the wide-spread demand for recall and those of us who believe that that would be a great misfortune are bound to make the legal remedy, in which is opportunity for the public official to require proof, be confronted with the witnesses and to have opportunity to cross-examine and give his evidence and have judicial judgment — make that so adequate that we will hear no more of this demand for recall.

I have sat for weeks in the trial of an impeachment case, feeling that the injury to the interests of the people of the country through the stoppage of the wheels of government in order to listen to a large mass of testimony that I knew would not be disputed, made it hardly worth while to get rid of the unfaithful official.

This provision is one which will permit every really important witness to be heard before the court. Of course, if a showing is made, if a suggestion is made, that a particular witness is a critical one, that counsel want court to see him and hear him when he testifies, then order the testimony to be taken before him. But the great body of testimony is not of that character. Of course, counsel for the defense requires the other side to prove their entire case, whether they have any idea of controversy over the proof or not, and it is that great mass of routine, customary, but obligatory testimony which ought to be taken by a commission composed of members of the court and reporting, so that the great mass, the great body of the chief legislative assembly of the state and of the judges of the Court of Appeals shall not be obliged to waste their time while it is being taken.

It seems to me that this is a practical, sensible piece of government business, for us to make this method of dealing with unfaithful officials more available and useful. I hope the amendment will prevail.

ON ENDING THE SCANDAL OF THE LAW'S DELAYS

ADDRESS OF AUGUST 19, 1915

Article VIII of the proposed constitution dealt with the judiciary, and section 6 thereof was entitled the Civil Practice Act. This section made it the duty of the legislature to act with all convenient speed upon the report of the Board of Statutory Consolidation transmitted to the legislature on April 21, 1915, and to enact a brief and simple civil practice act and to adopt a separate body of civil practice rules for the regulation of procedure in the Court of Appeals, the Supreme Court and county courts. Secondly, at intervals of not less than five years the legislature was authorized to appoint a commission to consider and report what changes, if any, there should be in the law and rules governing civil procedure. Further, the legislature was forbidden to " enact any law prescribing, regulating, or changing the civil procedure in the Court of Appeals, Supreme Court, or county courts, unless the Judges or Justices empowered to make and amend civil practice rules shall certify that legislation is necessary." It was finally declared that after the adoption of the civil practice rules by the legislature the power to alter and amend such rules and to make, alter and amend civil practice rules should vest and remain in the courts of the state, to be exercised by the judges of the Court of Appeals and the justices of the Appellate Division of the Supreme Court or by such judges or justices of the Court of Appeals, the Supreme Court and the county courts as the legislature might provide.

When this section of the constitution was under consideration in the Committee of the Whole, Mr. Root delivered the following address:

I WANT to say a few words which are stirred up by the appeal to memory by the gentleman from Saratoga.

I remember the conditions which existed prior to the adoption of the Civil Procedure Act of 1875, going back a good many years before. I was in the thick of the controversy long before Montgomery Throop changed it in his great tome which was called *The Code of Civil Procedure,* and the controversy was between the old common-law practice and the advocates of the reform procedure which went all over the country. That reform was accomplished under the express direction of the constitution of 1846. . . .

Under the old common-law system practice had become so complicated and difficult that it was hard for an honest man to get his rights. There is a good deal of human nature in that. It has been so since the laws of the Medes and Persians were formulated; it has been so since the day of Egypt's power. Wherever a special class of men have been entrusted with the formulation and administration of law, they tend to make it a mystery; they tend to become more and more subtle and refined in their discriminations, until ultimately they have got out of the field where they can be followed up by plain, honest people's minds, and some power must be exerted to bring them back. The constitution of 1846 exerted that power to bring the practice of the law out of the discredit into which it had fallen because of the intricacy and the complication and the technicality and the subtlety of the old common-law practice. Mr. Field brought it back with the code, of three hundred and odd sections, which bears his name, and the reform in procedure went all over the country. Curiously enough, just about the time that England followed the example and adopted the reformed procedure in her Judicature Act of 1873, we began to take a back track and Mr. Throop's attempt to condense in a volume which was called *The Code of Civil Procedure* a great number of particular and minute provisions regarding practice was the first great step in that direction, in the backward direction.

Now, in the forty years which have elapsed, we have been following in that same pathway until the people of our state have come to regard the simplification of practice as one of the great issues of the day. I believe there is no duty which is demanded from this convention more generally than the duty to do something to make our practice more simple, speedy, inexpensive, and effective. Why is it? A careful study of it reveals the cause, or the principal cause. I have listened to discussions and have taken part in them in the Bar Association of my own city, in the State Bar Association, in the American Bar Association, in countless conversations with lawyers and with laymen, and I say the cause of the prevailing discontent with our practice is to be found in the fact that year by year during all this period of forty years, there has been a continual addition, step by step, statute by statute, to the multitude of definite, certain, precise rules of procedure, binding upon the men that seek redress of wrongs in the courts. One of our most honored and beloved judges in the Court of Appeals said to me the other day, when I asked him how he thought this plan would work, " I have had since I came here to buy fifteen editions of the *Code* because it is so continually changed that after every session of the legislature my last edition is useless," and he gave this plan his warm approval.

The trouble is not in a particular provision. These provisions that are put in are put in with good intent. The men who propose them in the legislature are honest men who believe that they are useful, but they are not the result of any general view of the subject. They are the result of particular views of the needs of particular cases; and a provision that a member of the assembly or the senate may well honestly believe to be useful upon his experience in a particular case, may work very badly, interfering with the obtaining of justice in many other different cases. And when you come to put them all together, you have a great variety of statutory rights. Each one of these is a statutory right. I heard the other day a lawyer in New York boast that he could postpone any litigation for seven years, and I asked a lot of friends as I came along whether that was true, and they all said they did not doubt it. How ? Why, by compelling the honest fellow that comes into court to redress a wrong or to secure a right, to litigate one after the other these statutory rights that have been created by the legislature. Courts cannot ignore them because they are rights given by law. The courts must observe the law, and so the plain man who wants to get a wrong redressed has, bristling between his demand for redress and his judgment a dozen litigations that he has to fight out before he can get to the end of his cause.

My friends of the bar, we have been making our system of procedure here conform to the subtle, acute, highly-trained ideas of lawyers. That is not the true basis. The system of procedure, of course, cannot be simple, but as far as possible, it ought to be made to conform to the plain man's intelligence and experience. It ought to be so that the farmer and the merchant and the laborer can understand it, and know why he is delayed in getting his rights; can understand that the processes to which he is subject have a reason and know what the reason is, otherwise you cannot have that respect for the law, that confidence in its justice necessary for the maintenance of a system of just administration. And furthermore the existence of this great variety of minute, detailed statutory provisions has been breeding up a great number of code lawyers, and by that I mean lawyers whose principal concern is with the statutory code of rights and not with getting justice for their clients.

Now, we ought to get back, get back to the fundamental idea of our profession which is the administration of justice. These minute, particular code provisions substitute rules, multitudes of rules for the justice of the particular case. I agree with Mr. Brackett. I am old enough at the bar to have the men who were my partners, my juniors, my clerks, sitting on the bench, and I look at them from a different angle from that which I can recall forty or fifty years ago when I looked up to those men high up above — they are men like the rest of us. But, my friends, they are honest and just. They want to do justice if they can be permitted to.

They will do justice if they are permitted to. This network of meticulous rules that are made by our legislature with honest purpose prevent them from doing justice in the particular case; and the people of our state and of our country understand this. They may not understand the details. They may not know why, but they feel that the pathway of justice is obstructed. They feel that the honest man would better lose his claim than go into court and spend his time and money in the law's pursuit which seems to have no end. And they are indignant over it and restless and dissatisfied over it, and they look to us to do something. Now, what is it ? What can we do ? I can assure you that I have done the best I could for years to try to find some formula, some method by which the thing that the constitutional convention of 1846 did could be done again, for by a different route we have come into the same condition with which they dealt and after most earnest thought, particularly as the result of the discussions in all these bar associations, I have not found anything that offered so much light as the proposal of our judiciary committee.

It is not simple, but show us something better. We must do something. We cannot go home and say to our friends and neighbors we have given you no relief in this matter that concerns you so deeply.

Show us something better than that. What is it ? In the first place it requires the legislature to act upon this report of the commission on statutory consolidation. It does not say how they shall act. We don't undertake to interfere with them in that.

In the second place, it requires them to pass some sort of a brief civil practice act and adopt some sort of rules of procedure; it requires these two divisions. That is following what our neighboring state of Connecticut has adopted. They have a practice act that you can fold up and put in your side pocket. When the legislature in its wisdom has done that, then two results are provided, one is that the legislature shall stop the eternal tinkering with the practice, stop passing laws which are brought in here by individual members upon a narrow view of the occasion for them; shall stop every year pouring out a stream of amendments, and making new rules to cure the evils of old rules, and shall confine its action to periodical action upon the report of a commission. I agree with the idea that the legislature itself has not the time to elaborate and work out a system. It has too many other things to do. Accordingly the practice has become quite universal of having commissions appointed which shall prepare and present to the legislature well-considered measures. The legislature is given the fullest power; that is, it retains the fullest power to act upon reforms. It does not have to follow the recommendation of the commission. When the commission has reported, the legislature can throw their recommendation out the window if it sees fit; but the action of the legislature is concentrated on the point where it has the report before it, so that it will act upon the subject and not upon the ideas of A today and B tomorrow and C the day after, upon particular rules but it will act upon a system of practice as a whole, upon the report of a commission of its own selection, and it will act once for all until another period has elapsed, and so you stop this meticulous interference with practice, and you have an opportunity to test the provisions which the legislature adopts from time to time on the reports of its commissions. In the meantime the courts are authorized to proceed with their immemorial function of amending and adjusting the rules subject to the practice act of the legislature so that they will contribute to the doing of justice in the individual case and discourage these technicalities and subtleties which tangle justice in the net of form.

Now, there is nothing that cannot be criticised; nothing that cannot be doubted. Of course the judges when they come to make their rules may make rules that Mr. Wickersham would approve and Mr. Brackett would disapprove, or it may be just the other way. But if the judges make rules or amendments to the rules that do not on the whole seem to be right, at the next period, when the legislature takes the subject up, it will put into its practice act a provision that will control the bad rule. This provision reported by the committee is highly meritorious in that it compels the legislature to act in the broad way upon procedure as a whole, and at the same time it enables the legislature to control and correct any tendencies by the court to go wrong in either direction. I have seen and heard of no proposal to accomplish the thing that we clearly must accomplish which seems to be so effective as that proposed by the committee.

COURTS OF JUSTICE FOR SMALL CAUSES

ADDRESS OF AUGUST 23, 1915

The convention having under consideration section 8 of the proposed constitution, relating to the judiciary, and a discussion having arisen as to the territorial jurisdiction and powers of the City Court of the City of New York, Mr. Root said:

I AM not familiar with the situation to which this particular provision applies. I would like to make an observation upon the general subject to which this provision belongs.

It requires continual watchfulness to preserve the courts of small jurisdiction for the trial of the causes of the poor, of men of moderate means, of small business. Their causes are more important to them than the great causes which receive the attention of the press and enlist the services of leaders of the bar in the great courts. Every time, however, that you create a court for the trial of small causes the court immediately sets to work to get its jurisdiction enlarged. It never fails. I speak upon the careful attention growing out of the consideration of this same subject in the judiciary committee of the convention twenty-one years ago. Every court created for the trial of small causes tries to get its jurisdiction enlarged, and when the jurisdiction is enlarged the judges give their attention to the larger causes and neglect the small causes. They would rather be concerned in great affairs than in small affairs; and so, yielding in a good-natured way to the importunities of those gentlemen who wish to enlarge their offices, we gradually destroy court after court intended for the trial of small causes.

I think it was a mistake to increase the jurisdiction of this court from $2,000 to $5,000. I think it would be another mistake to give it full equity jurisdiction. You have got a of leaving public service corporations unregulated, except by the passage of laws in the legislature.

The public service commissions, both in this state and in other states and in the nation, were created to meet and deal with very great and real evils. In this state before we had that system, if a man was unjustly treated by a railroad, he had no recourse, except a lawsuit that was beyond his means, or a complaint to his representative in the legislature. A lawsuit by a single individual of moderate means against one of these great corporations was hopeless. The complaint to his representative in the legislature would result in the introduction of a bill founded upon, perhaps, just complaint, and those bills accumulated. A great deal of the time of the legislature was taken up by them.

The duty of holding these corporations accountable was a burden upon the legislature which it ought not to have been called upon to perform. But, worse than that, this multitude of bills, founded upon just complaint, brought after them a multitude of strike bills introduced for the purpose of holding up the corporations, holding them up and calling them down.

Many of us can now remember the dreadful days of the "Black Horse Cavalry" which came as an incident mainly, to the performance of this duty by the legislature. Further still, the fact that the great transportation companies were being attacked, the great public service corporations were being attacked in the legislature, justified them in their own minds in going into politics and electing, or furnishing the money to elect, members of the senate and assembly. Good men, good citizens, honest, law-abiding men justified themselves in the directorates of these railroads and other public service corporations in spending the money of the corporation to elect senators and assemblymen who would protect them against strike bills. The whole system became a scandal and a disgrace, and it was to remedy that here in New York and all over the country that this system of regulation by a commission created by law was established.

The results have been most beneficent. No greater reform has been wrought in the public life of our country than has been wrought by the transfer of this attempt to regulate these great corporations from the legislative bodies of the country to public service commissions. Now if a poor fellow is injured by a railroad company, he has somebody to go to, and the company can be held accountable. Now there is no cloud of strike bills in the legislature. Now there is no justification for the New York Central or the Erie or the Delaware and Hudson or the electric light companies or the telegraph or telephone companies to go into politics and spend their money with the idea that they must protect themselves in the legislature.

We can regard with greater respect the government of our state than we could. We never should permit a return to the old and vicious system. We should not now lose the opportunity to make the return impossible, because men forget. The generation that knew the old, evil days of the "Black Horse Cavalry" is passing away, and when it is gone a new generation which knows not the cause for the creation of this system will arise; and, ignorant of the evils to which they would be returning by destroying it, they may wipe it out. So I hope that we, who know the reason for the creation of this system of regulation by commission will put into this constitution enough, just enough, to make it impossible for any legislature ever to destroy it and return to the old, evil days, leaving the real legislation for the further development of the system to the legislature.

INVISIBLE GOVERNMENT

SPEECH ON THE SHORT BALLOT AMENDMENT, AUGUST 30, 1915

In the states of the American Union, most of the public officers are elected by popular vote. As candidates for the elective positions are nominated by the different parties, and as the names of all the candidates are printed on one and the same ballot, the ordinary voter finds himself in the presence of many names, among which he must select if he wishes the election of a particular person instead of the election of the party ticket. The idea of the so-called short ballot is to restrict the number of officers to be elected by the people at any one election, in order that the voters may concentrate their attention upon a few candidates and thus select those believed to be best qualified for the positions; to allow the officers thus elected to appoint other public officers, and to hold the elected officers responsible not only for their own conduct, but for the selection and conduct of their appointees. It is believed by the advocates of the short ballot that by this method some of the evils of what has come to be called " Invisible Government " will be eliminated.

In behalf of the short ballot, and of honest, open government, Mr. Root delivered the following address:

I HAVE had great doubt whether or not I should impose any remarks on this bill upon the convention, especially after my friend, Mr. Quigg, has so ingeniously made it difficult for me to speak; but I have been so long deeply interested in the subject of the bill, and I shall have so few opportunities hereafter, perhaps never another, that I cannot refrain from testifying to my faith in the principles of government which underlie the measure, and putting upon this record, for whatever it may be worth, the conclusions which I have reached upon the teachings of long experience in many positions, through many years of participation in the public affairs of this state and in observation of them.

I wish, in the first place, to say something suggested by the question of my friend, Mr. Brackett, as to where this short ballot idea came from. It came up out of the dark, he says.

Let us see. In 1910, Governor Hughes, in his annual message, said this to the legislature of the state: " There should be a reduction in the number of elective offices. The ends of democracy will be better attained to the extent that the attention of the voters may be focussed upon comparatively few offices, the incumbents of which can be strictly accountable for administration. This will tend to promote efficiency in public office by increasing the effectiveness of the voter and by diminishing the opportunities of political manipulators who take advantage of the multiplicity of elective offices to perfect their schemes at the public expense. I am in favor of as few elective offices as may be consistent with proper accountability to the people, and a short ballot. It would be an improvement, I believe, in state administration if the executive responsibility was centered in the governor, who should appoint a cabinet of administrative heads accountable to him and charged with the duties now imposed upon elected state officers."

Following that message from Governor Hughes, to whom the people of this state look with respect and honor, a resolution for the amendment to the constitution was introduced in the Assembly of 1910. That resolution provided for the appointment of all state officers, except the governor and the lieutenant-governor.

There was a hot contest upon the floor. Speaker Wadsworth, came down from the speaker's chair to advocate the measure, and Jesse Phillips, sitting before me, voted for it. And so, in the practical affairs of this state, the movement out of which this bill came had its start upon the floor of the state legislature.

Hughes and Wadsworth, one drawing from his experience as governor and the other upon his observation of public affairs, from the desk of the speaker of the assembly, were its sponsors.

Time passed, and in 1912 the movement had gained such headway among the people of the state that the Republican convention of that year declared its adherence to the principle of the short ballot, and the Progressive convention, in framing its platform, under which two hundred thousand — it is safe, is it not, to say two hundred thousand — of the Republican voters of this state followed Roosevelt as their leader, rather than Taft; the Progressive convention, in framing its platform, declared: " We favor the short ballot principle and appropriate constitutional amendments."

So two parties, and all branches of the Republican party at least, committed themselves to the position that Hughes and Wadsworth took, in the Assembly of 1910.

In 1913, after the great defeat of 1912, when the Republicans of the state were seeking to bring back to their support the multitudes that had gone off with the Progressive movement; when they were seeking to offer a program of constructive forward movement in which the Republican party should be the leader, Republicans met in a great mass meeting in the city of New York, on the fifth of December of that year, 1913.

Nine hundred and seventy Republicans were there from all parts of the state. It was a crisis in the affairs of the Republican party. The party must commend itself to the people of the state, or it was gone. Twenty-eight members of this convention were there, and in that meeting, free to all, open to full discussion, after amendments had been offered, discussed and voted upon, this resolution was adopted:

WHEREAS, This practice [referring to the long ballot] is also in violation of the best principles of organization which require that the governor, who under the constitution is the responsible chief executive should be so in fact, and that he should have the power to select his official agents;

Therefore, be it *Resolved*, that we favor the application to the state government of the principle of the short ballot, which is that only those offices should be elective which are important enough to attract (and deserve) public examination.

And be it further *Resolved*, that, in compliance with this principle, we urge the representatives of the Republican party of this state, in the senate and assembly, to support a resolution providing for the submission to the people of an amendment to the constitution, under which amendment it will be the duty of the governor to appoint the secretary of state, the state treasurer, the comptroller, the attorney-general, and the state engineer and surveyor, leaving only the governor and lieutenant-governor as elective state executive officers.

That resolution, I say, after full discussion was unanimously adopted by the nine hundred and seventy representative Republicans who had met there to present to the people of the state a constructive program for the party. Mr. Frederick C. Tanner is chairman of this Committee on Governor and Other State Officers today, because it was he who offered the resolution in that meeting that was unanimously approved by those nine hundred and seventy Republicans. He is executing a mandate. He is carrying out a policy. He is fulfilling a pledge to the people.

The time went on and the following winter, in the Assembly of 1914, a new resolution was introduced following the terms of this resolution of the mass meeting, following the terms of the Hughes-Wadsworth resolution of 1910, providing that all these state officers except the governor and lieutenant-governor should be appointed. That resolution passed the assembly and every Republican in the assembly voted for it. It never came to a vote in the senate. Voting for that resolution were four members of the assembly, who now sit in this convention: Mr. Bockes, Mr. Eisner, Mr. Hinman, and Mr. Mathewson.

Time passed on and in the autumn of 1914 a Republican convention met at Saratoga; an unofficial convention, we are told. Unofficial? Negligible! Here is the law under which it was called, Section 45 of the election law:

Nothing contained in this chapter shall prevent a party from holding party conventions to be constituted in such manner and to have such powers in relation to formulating party platforms and policies and the transaction of business relating to party affairs as the rules and regulations of the party may provide, not inconsistent with the provisions of this chapter.

That convention was thus called more specifically and solemnly to frame a platform than any other convention that ever met in this state, for that was its sole business. That is what it was there for; to define, to declare, to set before the people the faith and policies of the Republican party; and in that convention there was a report from the Committee on Rules, which embodied deliberation, full discussion and mature judgment, such as no report that ever came to a political convention within my experience ever had. The great mass meeting of December 5, 1913, had directed the appointment of a Committee of Thirty to meet and consider and prepare for submission to the convention a statement of the views of the Republican party regarding the new constitution. That committee was appointed; it met two or three days before the convention in the city of Saratoga. It met in the office of my friend, Mr. Brackett, and there day after day it discussed the subject, reached and voted upon its conclusions and framed a report.

Let me say here, that Senator Brackett never agreed with the committee. He has been consistent and honest and open in the declaration of his views from first to last, but he was voted down in the Committee of Thirty. Their report favoring a short ballot, among other things, was presented to the convention. That report was referred to the Committee on Resolutions of the convention, a committee of forty-two members, among them twelve members of this convention, and that Committee on Resolutions took up the report of the Committee of Thirty and discussed it all day and they voted upon it, and again Mr. Brackett's view was voted down; and the Committee on Resolutions reported to the convention the plank in favor of the short ballot that has been read to you.

Mr. BRACKETT. Will the Senator permit an interruption? I know you have not intentionally made a misstatement, but you will recall that a report of the Committee of Thirty was not presented to the Committee on Platform until an hour before the convention, in the little room at the end of the piazza — before the convention met.

Mr. ROOT. It is a fact, and that room was the scene of excited and hot controversy for a long period over the adoption of that report, which was in part adopted and in part rejected.

Mr. BRACKETT. If you will pardon a suggestion, you said for a long period. It was, I think, about an hour and a half.

Mr. DEYO. Will the gentleman give way? I think that lasted until the following day.

Mr. ROOT. It did.

When it came to the convention, there was no doubt about the subject we were talking on. The temporary chairman of the convention had said to the convention, "The reflections which arise from considering the relations of the executive and the legislature lead inevitably to another field of reform in state government. That is, the adoption of the short ballot. That is demanded both for the efficiency of our electoral system, and for the efficiency of government after election." And then, after stating the first, he proceeded: "The most obvious step toward simplifying the ballot in this state is to have the heads of executive departments appointed by the governor, etc. Still more important would be the effect of such a change upon the efficiency of government. The most important thing in constituting government is to unite responsibility with power, so that a certain known person may be definitely responsible for doing what ought to be done; to be rewarded if he does it and punished if he does not do it, and that the person held responsible shall have the power to do the thing. Under our system we have divided executive power among many separately elected heads of departments, and we have thus obscured responsibility, because in the complicated affairs of our government it is hard for the best informed to know who is to be blamed, or who is to be praised, who ought to be rewarded or who punished. At the same time that the governor is empowered to appoint the heads of executive departments and made responsible for their conduct, there plainly ought to be a general reorganization of the executive branch of our government."

After that, Mr. Chairman, came the report of the Committee on Resolutions, and Mr. Brackett submitted a minority report, taking substantially the position which he has taken here. That minority report was read, and it was argued at length. Amendments were offered and discussed. Mr. Brackett, I repeat, was heard at length upon it, in what he then called the " great council of the party ", and he was beaten; beaten fighting manfully for his opinions, but he was beaten. The Republican party went to the people at the coming election upon the declaration that it was in favor of applying the principle of the short ballot to the selection of executive officers.

Let me turn to the other side of the story. When the resolution for the short ballot, simon-pure, making all the state officers but the governor and lieutenant-governor appointive, was before the Assembly of 1914, Mr. A. E. Smith, the member of this convention whose attractive personality has so impressed itself upon every member, moved an amendment to limit the change to appointment of the secretary of state, state engineer and surveyor and state treasurer, leaving the comptroller and attorney-general elective. Upon that amendment the Democrats of the assembly stood, voting with him. When the Democratic convention met in that autumn they put themselves on Mr. Smith's platform, approved his action and that of the Democrats in the assembly and declared in favor of exactly what he called for in his amendment — the election of the comptroller and the attorney-general and the appointment of all the other officers.

So you have this movement, not coming up out of the dark, but begun by a great Governor and advocated by a great Speaker, both of whom have received the approval of their country, one by being elevated to the bench of the Supreme Court of the United States and the other to the Senate of the United States. You have the movement progressing step by step until it has received the almost universal assent, the final and decisive action of the party to which that Governor and that Speaker belong, repeated over and over and over again, fully thought out and discussed; and you have the other party accepting the principle, agreeing to the application of it, with the exception of the comptroller and the attorney-general.

Now, we must vote according to our consciences. We are not bound — no legislative body is bound legally by a platform. But, Mr. Chairman, if there is faith in parties, if there is ever to be a party platform put out again, to which a man can subscribe or for which he can vote without a sense of futility, without a sense of being engaged in a confidence game; if all the declarations of principle by political parties are not to be regarded as false pretense, as humbug, as a parcel of lies, we must stand by the principles upon which we were all elected to this convention. There is one thing, and, in so far as I know, only one thing, that the vast majority of us have assured the people who elected us we would do in this convention, and that is that we would stand by the position of Hughes and Wadsworth. I, for one, am going to do it. If I form a correct judgment of the self-respecting men of this convention, it will be with a great company that I do it.

But, Mr. Chairman, do not let us rest on that. Why was it that these conventions, one after another, four of them, declared to the people that they were for the principle of this bill? In the first place, our knowledge of human nature shows us that the thousands of experienced men in these conventions and meetings had come to the conclusion that that principle met with the opinion of the people of the state. It is all very well for Mr. Quigg to tell us what the men he met in Columbia county said, for Mr. Green to write letters to his friends in Binghamton, but nine hundred and seventy men in that mass meeting on the fifth of December told you what their observation was, that they would commend their party to the people of this state by declaring this principle. A thousand and odd men in the Republican conventions of 1912, 1913, and 1914 have given proof conclusive of what their observation of public opinion was. A thousand and odd men in the Democratic convention of 1914 have given proof conclusive of what their observation of public opinion was. Conventions do not put planks in platforms to drive away votes.

Again I ask, why was it that they thought that these principles would commend their tickets to the people of the state? Why was it that the people of the state had given evidence to these thousands of experienced men in the politics of the state that those principles would be popular? Well, of course, you cannot escape the conclusion that it was because the people of the state found something wrong about the government of the state. My friend, Mr. Brackett, sees nothing wrong about it. He has been for fifteen years in the Senate; I suppose he could have stayed there as long as he wanted to. He is honored and respected and has his own way in Saratoga county. Why should he see anything wrong? My friend, Mr. Green, is comfortably settled in the Excise Department, and he sees nothing wrong. Mr. Chairman, there never was a reform in administration in this world which did not have to make its way against the strong feeling of good, honest men, concerned in existing methods of administration, and who saw nothing wrong. Never! It is no impeachment to a man's honesty, his integrity, that he thinks the methods that he is familiar with and in which he is engaged are all right. But you cannot make any improvement in this world without overriding the satisfaction that men have in the things as they are, and of which they are a contented and successful part. I say that the growth, extension, general acceptance of this principle shows that all these experienced politicians and citizens in all these conventions felt that the people of the state saw something wrong in our state government, and we are here charged with a duty, not of closing our eyes, but of opening them, and seeing, if we can, what it was that was wrong.

Anybody can see that all these one hundred and fifty-two outlying agencies, big and little, lying around loose, accountable to nobody, spending all the money they can get, violate every principle of economy, of efficiency, of the proper transaction of business. Every one can see that all around us are political organizations carrying on the business of government, that have learned their lesson from the great business organizations which have been so phenomenally successful in recent years.

The governments of our cities: why, twenty years ago, when James Bryce wrote his *American Commonwealth*, the government of American cities was a byword and a shame for Americans all over the world. Heaven be thanked, the government of our cities has now gone far toward redeeming itself and us from that disgrace, and the government of American cities today is in the main far superior to the government of American states. I challenge contradiction to that statement. How has it been reached? How have our cities been lifted up from the low grade of incompetency and corruption on which they stood when the *American Commonwealth* was written? It has been done by applying the principles of this bill to city government, by giving power to the men elected by the people to do the things for which they were elected. But I say it is quite plain that that is not all. It is not all.

I am going to discuss a subject now that goes back to the beginning of the political life of the oldest man in this convention, and one to which we cannot close our eyes, if we keep the obligations of our oath. We talk about the government of the constitution. We have spent many days in discussing the powers of this and that and the other officer. What is the government of this state? What has it been during the forty years of my acquaintance with it? The government of the constitution? Oh, no; not half the time, nor half way. When I ask what do the people find wrong in our state government, my mind goes back to those periodic fits of public rage in which the people rouse up and tear down the political leader, first of one party and then of the other party. It goes back to the public feeling of resentment against the control of party organizations, of both parties and of all parties.

Now, I treat this subject in my own mind not as a personal question to any man. I am talking about the system. From the days of Fenton, and Conkling, and Arthur, and Cornell, and Platt, from the days of David B. Hill, down to the present time, the government of the state has presented two different lines of activity, one of the constitutional and a view to the service that can be given to the public. The other, the false one, looks upon appointment to office with a view to what can be gotten out of it.

Gentlemen of the convention, I appeal to your knowledge of facts. Every one of you knows that what I say about the use of patronage under the system of invisible government is true. Louis Marshall told us the other day about the appointment of wardens in the Adirondacks, hotel keepers and people living there, to render no service whatever. They were appointed not for the service that they were to render to the state; they were appointed for the service they were to render to promote the power of a political organization. Mr. Chairman, we all know that the halls of this capitol swarm with men during the session of the legislature on pay day. A great number, seldom here, rendering no service, are put on the payrolls as a matter of patronage, not of service, but of party patronage. Both parties are alike; all parties are alike. The system extends through all. Ah, Mr. Chairman, that system finds its opportunity in the division of powers, in a six-headed executive, in which, by the natural workings of human nature, there shall be opposition and discord and the playing of one force against the other; and so, when we refuse to make one governor elected by the people the real chief executive, we make inevitable the setting up of a chief executive not selected by the people, not acting for the people's interest, but for the selfish interest of the few who control the party, whichever party it may be.

Think for a moment of what this patronage system means. How many of you are there who would be willing to do to your private client, or customer, or any private trust, or to a friend or neighbor, what you see being done to the state of New York every year of your lives in the taking of money out of her treasury without service? We can, when we are in a private station, pass on without much attention to inveterate abuses. We can say to ourselves, I know it is wrong, I wish it could be set right; it cannot be set right, I will do nothing. But here, here, we face the duty, we cannot escape it, we are bound to do our work, face to face, in clear recognition of the truth, unpalatable, deplorable as it may be, and the truth is that what the unerring instinct of the democracy of our state has seen in this government is, that a different standard of morality is applied to the conduct of affairs of state than that which is applied in private affairs. I have been told forty times since this convention met that you cannot change it. We can try, can we not? I deny that we cannot change it. I repel that cynical assumption which is born of the lethargy that comes from poisoned air during all these years. I assert that this perversion of democracy, this robbing democracy of its virility, can be changed as truly as the system under which Walpole governed the commons of England, by bribery, as truly as the atmosphere which made the *Crédit Mobilier* scandal possible in the Congress of the United States, has been blown away by the force of public opinion. We cannot change it in a moment, but we can do our share. We can take this one step toward, not robbing the people of their part in government, but toward robbing an irresponsible autocracy of its indefensible and unjust and undemocratic control of government, and restoring it to the people to be exercised by the men of their choice and their control.

Mr. Chairman, this convention is a great event in the life of every man in this room. A body which sits but once in twenty years to deal with the fundamental law of the state, deals not only for the present but for the future, not only by its results but by its example. Opportunity knocks at the door of every man in this assemblage, an opportunity which will never come again to most of us. While millions of men are fighting and dying for their countries across the ocean, while government is become serious, sober, almost alarming in its effect upon the happiness of the lives of all that are dearest to us, it is our inestimable privilege to do something here in moving our beloved state along the pathway towards better and purer government, a more pervasive morality and a more effective exercise of the powers of government which preserve the liberty of the people. When you go back to your homes and recall the record of the summer, you will find in it cause for your children and your children's children, who will review the convention of 1915 as we have been reviewing the work of the preceding conventions, to say: my father, my grandfather, helped to do this work for our state.

Mr. Chairman, there is a plain old house in the Oneida hills, overlooking the valley of the Mohawk, where truth and honor dwelt in my youth. When I go back, as I am about to go, to spend my declining years, I mean to go with the feeling that I have not failed to speak and to act here in accordance with the lessons I learned there from the God of my fathers. God grant that this opportunity for service to our country and our state may not be neglected by any of the men for whom I feel so deep a friendship in this convention.

SPEECH ON CLOSING THE CONVENTION

SEPTEMBER 10, 1915

At the closing session of the convention of 1915, and after delivery of the address below, the following tribute to Mr. Root, as its presiding officer, was unanimously adopted:

Resolved, That the thanks of this convention be tendered to the Honorable Elihu Root for the ability, fairness and courtesy which have distinguished his services as president of this convention.

OUR work is done. The long, hard months during which we have been wrestling with questions of government, and character has been struggling with character in the discussions of the proposed amendments to the constitution, are over. We have produced a revised constitution which is not a model of style, of form, of brevity, of theoretical perfection. Any one of us with the models which are available, could have produced in the solitude of his own office a more perfect and harmonious scheme of government; but this instrument is fitted by patience, experience, knowledge and effort, to the actual conditions of the life of a people which has been growing for three centuries, of a people living one half upon the sea and the other half in the river valleys and among the hills and on the shores of the Great Lakes, of a people of ten million with varied industries and interests and prepossessions and prejudices and sympathies; and to know the full meaning of all the provisions which this instrument contains one must have studied and know the life of the people of all the great state of New York. When we came to our work on the sixth of April last, we addressed ourselves first to studying the conditions of the government of the state. We found that there were serious evils which had resulted in an enormous increase of expenses from twelve million dollars at the time of the last convention to forty-two million dollars at the time of our meeting; an enormous increase of indebtedness and an apparent impossibility of meeting all attempts to curtail expenses or to prevent the further accumulation of debt. Upon further inquiry we found that the executive and administrative organization of the state was loose, confused, ill-regulated; that one hundred and fifty and more separate agencies were going about the business of government, responsible to no one in particular, each one spending all the money that it could get, and there was no such concentration of responsibility and power as was necessary to bring to accountability the agencies of the state which were plunging our people into extravagance and debt. We found that the legislature of the state had declined in public esteem and that the majority of members of the legislature were occupying themselves chiefly in the promotion of private and local bills, of special interests, with which they came to Albany, private and local interests upon which apparently their reëlections to their positions depended, and which made them cowards, and demoralized the whole body. We found that the course of justice was slow and expensive and hindered by technicalities and subtleties which kept honest men out of their rights. We found that the great offices, the hundreds of offices of the state were swarming with men who held sinecures, who were put in their places for the benefit of particular organizations and not for the services that they were to render to the state. We have done our best to devise and adopt measures which will remedy these evils. When one's automobile acts strangely and goes wrong, one does not berate it or pass resolutions about it; one endeavors to put one's finger on the fault in the machinery and correct the fault. The capacity of a people for self-government is measured by their ability to create and maintain institutions that will govern. Without the institutions of government there can be no government, for the vote alone accomplishes nothing, but in the creation of an active agent. We were elected by the people of the state to overhaul the machinery of government, to ascertain if we could where in that complicated mechanism lay the fault that caused the evils under which they suffered. We have done the best we could. We have given our best brain, our best strength, our best devotion to the accomplishment of that duty and now we submit our work to the people of the state, and we ask of them only this: As we have been your loyal and devoted servants, doing your behest to the best of our ability, be loyal to us and give at least a presumption in favor of the work that we have done. If you find it wrong, reject it; but do not reject it upon light or unconsidered reasons, for it is the best that your representatives, elected by you, devoting themselves for all this long summer to the work, can do to cure the evils of your government.

There are two special things which I wish to say before the close of this convention. One is — and I would like to say it to every citizen of the state — one is that this convention has risen above the plane of partisan politics. It has refused to make itself or permit itself to be made the agency of party advantage except as faithful service for the state is a benefit to party. It has refused to engage in the play of politics. No caucus and no conference has marred the impartiality of our proceeding. No resolution has bound the judgment or conscience of any member of this convention. Our conception of our duty was to leave behind strife of party, and upon the higher plane of patriotism and love of country, to join all together, whatever our parties, in doing the best we could for the prosperity of our beloved state. One effect of this course of conduct on our part has been that the debates of this convention compare most favorably with the debates of any parliamentary body which has sat in deliberation during the lifetime of any man in this room. I have seen and heard the debates of many parliamentary bodies and never have I heard or read debates in which the matter was more relevant, the discussion more earnest and to the point, the attempts at display less conspicuous, the speeches for home consumption more infrequent, and real discussion, that real open, public discussion of a deliberative body, which is the essential process of free self-government, on a higher level than in this convention of the year 1915.

And another result of this course of conduct has been that the thirty-three measures adopted by the convention have been adopted by these astonishing votes: Twelve of the measures were adopted unanimously; twelve were adopted by majorities of more than ten to one; of the remaining nine, two were adopted by majorities of more than seven to one, two by majorities of more than four to one, two by majorities of more than three to one, and three by majorities of more than two to one. That, in an assemblage composed of two different and perennially conflicting parties was the result of common patriotic contributions by the members of both parties towards the perfection of measures in a convention which was doing its work with a sense of the dignity of the people it represented, and not for party advantage.

All the great measures of this convention were adopted not only by the votes, the affirmative votes of a majority of the Republicans but by the affirmative votes of a majority of the Democrats in the convention. The executive reorganization plan, commonly called the short ballot, was adopted by the votes of ninety-seven Republicans in the affirmative and fifteen in the negative, and of twenty-eight Democrats in the affirmative and fifteen in the negative. The budget, that great new departure in the finance of the state, was adopted by the affirmative vote of one hundred and one Republicans to two Republicans in the negative and of thirty-six Democrats in the affirmative to two in the negative. The city home rule bill was adopted by one hundred and two Republicans voting in the affirmative and two in the negative; by eighteen Democrats voting in the affirmative and fifteen in the negative. The county home rule bill, which completes the scheme, was adopted by ninety-one Republicans voting in the affirmative and nine in the negative; and thirty-seven Democrats voting in the affirmative and two in the negative.

The judiciary bill, that great measure which prescribes the reform in judicial procedure that in the best judgment of this convention will give the honest man the chance for his rights, was adopted by the affirmative vote of one hundred and three Republicans to one Republican in the negative and thirty-two Democrats to two Democrats in the negative. So that in substance, upon the great measures of this convention both parties of the state are united, both have given their suffrages in favor of the reforms that we propose.

One other thing I wish to say, and that is that similar evils to those we have found in our state government have been found in the governments of many other states. People of those states have had recourse to an abandonment or a partial abandonment of representative government. They have had recourse to the initiative and referendum and the recall, the recall of officers and the recall of decisions. In this convention we have offered the most irrefutable, concrete argument against those nostrums and patent medicines in government and in favor of the preservation of that representative government which is the chief gift of our race to freedom, by undertaking to reform representative government, instead of abandoning it and to make it worthy of its great function for the preservation of liberty.

This constitution is not a matter of little prejudices or oppositions. It is not a business to be decided accordingly as one is opposed to raising this salary or that, or to extending the workmen's compensation or restricting it, or to making a little change in this office or that. It is to be decided upon great lines for it is a great work. It is a great departure in government. It is the best that the men selected by the people of the Empire State, to do the work for them, can do towards rescuing the representative government of our fathers from the obloquy which has come upon it in recent years. These great measures of the reorganization of the executive, of the new method of state finances, of the relief of the legislature from those petty preoccupations of local and private bills, which have been destroying its morale, of the establishment of the privileges and blessings of local self-government for the cities and for the counties of the state, of reform in judicial procedure, all these are great measures which should appeal to a great people who are competent to maintain the perpetuity of representative self-government. And upon those great lines I feel assured you may be confident the people's verdict will be cast.

Now, gentlemen of the convention, I bid you farewell with assurance of respect and esteem and affection. We have labored long together in a common cause, and I am sure we shall all carry to our homes the inestimable reward of faithful service in the possession of a host of brothers, children of our common country, devoted to the same cause, and loving each other as brother Americans. So I declare the constitutional convention of the state of New York of the year 1915 to be adjourned without day.

A STUDY OF THE PROPOSED CONSTITUTION

ADDRESS AT A DINNER OF THE REPUBLICAN CLUB OF NEW YORK, OCTOBER 18, 1915

After the adjournment of the constitutional convention of 1915 on September 9, Mr. Root delivered a series of carefully prepared addresses before representative bodies, advocating the adoption of the constitution of the state as amended. Of this series, two have been selected for publication; the first delivered before the Republican Club of New York, October 18, 1915; the second a week later, before the Economic Club of New York.

I NEED not tell you, I cannot tell you, how deeply I am affected by this warmth of greeting and this assurance of the endurance of old friendship. It is just about twenty years since you did me the honor to make me the president of this club, immediately following the constitutional convention of 1894. And now, after twenty years of life, with its struggles, with its expense of energy, with all the writing of life into the history of our state and our country, we have come again to the close of another constitutional convention, and you are greeting me once again with the warmth and loyalty of friendship that forbids any man to say that the people of a republic are ungrateful, or that the generous emotions and the loyal sentiments of true friendship are not a mighty power, transcending the materialism and the selfishness in the race for advantage and for property and for fame in this Republic. We have met many times, my friends, following the standard of some admired and beloved leader; often we have fought together to carry the standard of the party to victory, often we have gathered resolution in defeat to advance again for victory in the next election. The interests of personality, of living issues that immediately and directly affect our own fortunes, and the welfare of our communities, have been with us plain, and clear, and vivid when we have met before. We have sought to make our friend our leader, governor or president; but now we have a cold, dry, uninteresting question: A constitution of the state, prolix and complicated, with matters of dull governmental machinery affected, little or nothing to cause excitement, little or nothing to awaken public interest; yet, my friends, the issue, the cold, dry, uninteresting issue that is before us now transcends the interest and the importance of any success of any man in any election for which we have striven. We have passed in America that happy period of youth in which we could make mistakes without suffering for them. We have passed that condition of simple governmental affairs when any one could do anything under any system, and the vast complication and difficulty of our government is pressing home upon the welfare and the happiness and the liberty of our people. The test of capacity for self-government is to be found in the people's ability to create institutions which will at once preserve liberty and maintain order.

For five months and something more, a body of men, elected by the people of the state of New York, two-thirds of them Republicans, some of them elected in the state at large, holding their places by over one hundred thousand majority, have been applying themselves and laboring to reach just conclusions of the utmost importance upon the government of the state. They have produced a constitution as the result of listening to many witnesses, of securing much advice, of long and thorough study, of complete and full discussion, of reconciliation of views, of subordination of the less important to the more important; and this has resulted in a revised constitution of the state. It is not a thing of shreds and patches, it is not a thing to be considered according to the individual predilections of this man or that upon this particular subject or the other; it is a whole, a complete rounded whole, and, as a whole, the determination of the people of the state upon it is the most grave and serious determination which the people of the state have had to meet in many a decade.

Let me, if I can within the brief limits possible to such an occasion, try to state what it is. When the constitutional convention delegates, whom you elected, addressed themselves to considering the government of the state, they found that there were serious defects in all three branches of our government.

Our judicial procedure was complicated, technical and full of subtleties, and with a multitude of statutory provisions relating to procedure, which made it difficult for a plain and honest man to come into court and get his rights. The procedure had been built up by year after year of separate and specific code provisions and code amendments, which, taken all together, have created a multitude of statutory rights in the way of procedure that make it almost impossible for a litigation to be brought to a prompt and inexpensive conclusion.

We found that the executive branch of our government was ill-compacted, confused, extravagant, subject to no effective control; over one hundred and fifty agencies, great and small, all over the state, were carrying on business, and were responsible, practically, to no one. Every one spent all the money he could get, every one acted in accordance with his own judgment. Good men, honest men, trying to do their duty, but none of them held to responsibility or subject to the effective control and limitations of inspection and supervision.

We found that the legislature had declined in public esteem; we found that the members of the legislature, a very large proportion of them, were going to Albany with local and private bills, and special interests which they wished to subserve, and that every man who had a special bill and a special interest was made a coward and prevented from doing his duty toward the general interests of the state.

We found that the continually increasing tendency of the legislature to exercise its powers for the playing of politics, was making our government the means of securing personal advantage, personal appointments to office, personal appropriations out of the treasury of the state; and we sought, with all sincerity and earnestness within our power, to find remedies for those evils in the three great departments of the state.

We sought to deal with one by requiring the legislature again, as the constitutional convention of 1846 did, to return to simplicity and effectiveness of procedure in the attainment of justice. We undertook to require the legislature to pass a brief and simple practice act, and sweep away all this great body of statutory rights in procedure and leave the regulation of the rules under the general provisions of the practice act to the courts, so that our judges on the bench would be permitted to do justice in the particular case, instead of making men run the gauntlet of these acute and subtle and technical barriers to the attainment of their rights, which have been a disgrace to the administration of justice in this state.

In the executive department, we sought to apply the rule of responsibility, and to give men who are elected by the people the power which would make it possible to hold them responsible. We undertook to condense all those one hundred and fifty-two agencies of the state into seventeen departments; we undertook to require that the overlapping and the interference, and the useless expenditure of money should be done away with, by putting all those agencies into a limited number of departments, under one head that would be responsible and that could be held responsible by the governor of the state who himself can be held responsible by the people of the state because they will have given him power upon which they can hold him responsible.

And we undertook to rehabilitate the legislature of the state, not by any one provision — that was impossible — but by a series of provisions, and that is the central idea of the whole constitutional scheme included in this revision. In the first place, we found the legislature making up the appropriation bills, making them up in the dark, with suggestions for appropriations coming to the committees in private, in secret, coming from every one, responsible or irresponsible, coming from the members of the legislature themselves, each one wanting something, each one trying to get something for his constituency, appropriation bills brought out late in the session, running along on the calendar until the close of the session, and then, under an emergency passage, not printed, not discussed, not understood, passed by the legislature, then the legislature adjourning and the governor left with thirty days in which to sit down in the privacy of his office, with a blue pencil, and control the action of the legislature. That system was a complete reversal of the true and traditional system of representative government, under which the representatives of the people are to hold the purse strings. The governor was made to hold the purse strings, and the representatives of the people, instead of controlling expenditure, ran pell-mell to increase it. We have reversed it. We have taken this procedure, which stood on its head, turned it around and stood it on its feet and we have required, first, the heads of all those departments, the seventeen of them, who are now to be responsible, in the place of the one hundred and fifty-two, we have required them to furnish the governor in ample time a statement of the needs of their departments, to arrange them in the order

And now when the members of the legislature come to Albany, they will have practically nothing to do but to attend to the public business, to deal with general laws of the state, to stand against extravagant expenditure in the appropriation bills. We have cut off the right of emergency messages, which had made the old provision of the constitution of 1894 prohibiting a bill from being passed until it had been for three days in print in its final form, of no avail, because there would come in an emergency message declaring that the public interests required the immediate passage of the bill.

We have cut off these messages so that now no bill can be passed at all until it has been in print, on the desks of the members of both houses, for three full days in its final form.

So we have taken away the temptation to rush things through in the rather discreditable hurly-burly of the closing days of the session — things that nobody knew anything about and that would not stand having anybody know anything about them.

And then we have required that the debates of the legislature shall be printed from day to day just as the debates in Congress are, and the debates in the British House of Commons are, and the debates in the French Chamber are; so that in the first place, the people of the state will know what the men at Albany are doing, and why they are doing it, and so that the legislature of our state will be an opportunity for an able young man to help himself along in a career. Who knows now,— who knows now why things are done at Albany ? Here and there, a newspaper prints something that is said, but the necessities of news service require the striking and the spectacular to be reported, and the dull and uninteresting, real debates, are never known; and as a result, the art of debate has gradually been declining in Albany. Now a young man, if this constitution is adopted, can go to Albany, and if he has anything in him, he can get credit for it, and service in the legislature will be a stepping-stone to preferment in a public career.

And we have taken away the temptation to trade in offices, the temptation to bind the governor of the state to all sorts of bargains by doing away with the requirement that all of his appointments be confirmed by the state senate. We have taken away the temptation to pass "ripper" bills by putting into the constitution a fixed statement as to the heads of the great departments of the state, so that they cannot be made the football of selfish politics, but must remain the great agencies of true and patriotic politics. We have made it possible for the legislature of our state to retrieve the good name of the state legislatures of our country; we have made it possible for the executive of our state to make true the declaration so long standing in our constitution that the executive power is vested in the governor, and to perform the duty so long required of the governor to take care that the laws are executed.

We have made it possible that our courts, which wish to do justice, and will do justice if they are permitted, shall give an honest man his rights as against all shysters whatsoever.

And that is all one comprehensive scheme. You cannot submit it section by section; it is a complete inter-related, thought-out whole, for the redemption of the government of our state from the ill-repute into which it has fallen, for doing away with the selfish playing of politics in the place of government; for the reduction of the extravagance and lavishness and lack of responsibility that has brought our expenditures up from twelve millions at the time of the last convention, to forty-two millions a year at the time of this convention; that has brought our debt up from seven millions to one hundred and eighty-six millions; that has made our highways and our canals and public works generally the vehicles for graft and robbery of the public.

Now, we may be wrong about some things, but, we are not wrong about the need. No one will challenge the need for an improvement in the government of our state. These men who worked all the five months of the spring and summer, may not have found the true solution; but it is an extraordinary circumstance that after long study and discussion and full and open debate, they came, after all the wide differences of opinion, to an amazing agreement. Twelve of the measures of the convention were adopted by unanimous vote. Twelve by a vote of more than ten to one, and the remaining nine by votes of more than seven to one, more than four to one, more than three to one, and but three measures by votes of only two to one. And I will undertake to say that the conclusions upon these grave and serious matters, the reform of the machinery of our state government, reached by these men, selected from among our people after their long study and discussion, with such unanimity, cannot be justly challenged upon five minutes' consideration. We may have been wrong, but the reasons thus far alleged for voting against the constitution, compared with the weight and seriousness of the matter which the constitution carries, and the great results which it seeks to accomplish, are trifling, unworthy of consideration, bear the marks of but little consideration, and seem rather to be a means of excusing an opposition which finds its real origin and cause in something besides the reasons suggested.

Now, gentlemen, the convention had a majority of two-thirds of Republicans in round numbers, two-thirds Republicans, and one-third Democrats. The Republican majority of the convention, after much discussion and some feeling, reached the conclusion that it could serve its party best by serving its state best, and invited the coöperation, welcomed the assistance of the Democratic minority. We put into that constitution the affirmative constructive program adopted by the Republican party of the state by the mass meeting held in this city on December 5, 1913, at which nearly one thousand Republicans from all over the state were present. We put into it the constructive program which was approved by the Republican convention at Saratoga, in 1914. We put into it also the agreement of the Democratic party upon many of the great measures of constructive statesmanship for which the Republican party had declared, and upon all the great measures of the convention: upon the home rule measures; upon the judiciary article; upon the reorganization of the executive department, commonly spoken of as the short ballot bill; upon the budget reform. Upon all the five, the six, great measures which make the body of that revised constitution, there was a vote not only of a majority of the Republicans, but a majority of the Democrats of the convention. Now, how can Republicans fail to vote for it? It is their work. It is their program. It is giving effect to their declarations. How can Democrats fail to vote for it? For their best, their best whom they sent to the convention assented to it; agreed to it; put their thought and effort into it. So many of the eminent, respected, honored Democrats of the state are for it; but I regret to say that there are some men who are so unwilling to see the constitution adopted which was the work of a convention having a Republican majority, that they are seeking to do what the constitutional convention refused to do; they are seeking to play politics with the constitution. We thought it was our duty to rise above partisan play of politics and to serve our state; to show that our party sought to gain only by serving the state, and so it was with the great majority of the Democrats in the convention; but these men, these men are seeking to defeat this constitution, in order that they may reverse the judgment of 1914 which put Republicans in control of the convention, hoping that they may have another convention in 1917 or 1918, that they will control.

Great as is the issue of the constitution, almost as great is the question whether the people of the state of New York can be controlled by that low and unpatriotic view of public duty. If they succeed, who will write the constitution in 1918? What will be in it? All these schemes of reform of our government will have been discredited. Not these things; oh, no, the people would have voted against them. What will be in it? Dare you think of it? Mr. Gompers is against the constitution. He was defeated in 1914. If he succeeds, and there is another convention, and he is elected, he will perhaps write the constitution. I can name a lot of others who think that they will write the constitution if they can defeat this one; but it will have none of this plan of reform, for that will have been defeated by the people. . . .

I am told that the great danger to this constitution lies in the possibility that men may not vote upon it at all. Of course it is very difficult to vote upon a complicated matter which took the convention five months to work out, upon such consideration as can be given to it by the ordinary business man, by the farmer or the storekeeper, or, indeed, by any one whose time is occupied in his own affairs. But if we are ever to have a reform of our state which conforms to the necessities of economy and efficiency and the preservation of liberty and order, if we are to keep pace with the learning of our time, as to the methods of transacting business, if we are to make the affairs of government as well administered as the affairs of the great business corporations, the people of the state must take interest enough in such a question as this, either to study it and form their own opinions upon it, or to give the benefit of the presumption to the men whom they elected to work out the problems and to find remedies. And I invoke from you, my friends, earnest and sincere effort to bring to the people of our city and our state an appreciation of the importance of the subject which is before them, and the importance of their acting upon it, and acting upon it wisely. The Republican Club never had a duty more serious and more clear; and if you will perform that duty in the spirit of your past, you will add new lustre to your history and gain new credit as patriots and make me, at least, your long-time friend and loyal associate, more proud than ever of being a member of the Republican Club of the City of New York.

THE NEW YORK CONSTITUTION AND REPRESENTATIVE GOVERNMENT

ADDRESS BEFORE THE ECONOMIC CLUB OF NEW YORK
OCTOBER 25, 1915

At its thirty-third meeting at the Hotel Astor, on October 25, Mr. Root was the guest of honor of the Economic Club of New York. Mr. William E. Wilcox, the chairman of the meeting, in introducing Mr. Root as the presiding officer of the recent convention to revise the constitution of the state of New York, said:

> We are glad indeed to welcome here the distinguished gentleman who has rendered such lasting service to the country in the important offices he has held. To no man in our generation is the country under a greater debt of gratitude for the unselfish devotion he has shown to the state and to the nation, than to our distinguished guest.

WHEN the constitutional convention, the result of whose labor is before you for your action as electors of the state of New York, assembled in Albany in April last, they found themselves holding a warrant of but weak potentiality, as comparatively few of the people of the state had voted for a convention. A very small majority of those who voted had cast their votes in the affirmative. Yet there was a duty imposed upon the members of the convention; and upon a survey of the field it seemed to them that there was something to be done; not merely the amendment here and there of specific provisions of the constitution of the state; not mending and patching in detail the provisions relating to the different departments of the state government, but of wide and serious importance.

We all knew, and the members of the convention felt, that throughout the American Union there was dissatisfaction with the workings of state government. In a large part of the states of the Union that dissatisfaction had found expression in a partial abandonment of the system of representative government. In a great many of the states the people had turned from the attempt to establish by their votes from year to year satisfactory state governments, which through the workings of their legislative, executive, and judicial branches, should do the popular will, maintain order, secure justice, and preserve liberty, and had sought to substitute other methods of attaining their purposes: the initiative, the compulsory referendum, the more sudden and instant control over administrative and other judicial officers through the recall, — direct legislation as distinguished from representative legislation. Some of us who felt that representative government was the greatest gift of our race to the development of freedom, some of us who had been standing for years in opposition to the abandonment of representative government, felt that in that convention the duty pressing upon us was to show, if we could, that instead of abandoning representative government because of its defects and the evils which accompanied its exercise, we should seek to cure the evils by improving representative government, and bringing it back to the exercise of its full power and the performance of its great function; and the effort to give to the people of the state of New York an improvement of representative government which should be an answer to all those who were preaching the abandonment of representative government, is the keynote of the work of the convention; is the reason and the rationale of the constitution which is before you now for action.

Of course, if legislation is to be direct, if the laws of the state or nation are to be made at the polls upon the initiative of any group of men who have ideas that they wish to propose, the dignity and the power of representative assemblies must decline. Of course, if that system of government is to prevail, the American system of government through representative assemblies must grow weaker and weaker; and if that system is not to prevail, representative assemblies must be made to do their work, to meet the well executed purpose and the will of the people whom they represent. It is that feature of the work of the convention which should, I think, appeal to this Economic Club; for you deal not merely with details, but with the philosophy of government, and with the broad, underlying principles which are to be applied. And I put to you, as the first great ground upon which the work of this convention is to be favorably regarded, that it is an effort, sincere and serious on the part of the one hundred and sixty-eight men elected by the people to do the work, to reinstate the representative government of our fathers in the position to which it is entitled, and to make it so good, so sound, so effective a government, that all demand for the abandoning of representative government and the substitution of direct legislation will pass away, and be repudiated.

Now, we found certain manifest defects in our government. They were not peculiar to the government of the state of New York. They are to be found throughout the Union, in the government of most, if not all, of the states. Although there was no great majority of the people calling for a constitution, the members of the convention deemed it their duty to deal with these defects.

Let me try, in the brief time I have, to state in outline what they were. In the first place, we found that under our judicial system the course of justice had come to be obstructed; it is slow and expensive and uncertain. It takes years for an honest man going into court to assert a right, or redress a wrong, to reach his conclusion. He finds himself obstructed, frustrated in the progress of his suit. If he reaches a favorable result, he finds himself sent back on appeal, and he is obliged to begin over again. Whenever the administration of justice is entrusted to a class and guild, the tendency always is to make it a mystery, to have it become more refined, and subtle, and technical; and as you understand the course of development of judicial procedure, you perceive that from time to time it has been necessary for the people, who want only simple justice, to step in and bring back the administration of their courts to their own simple basis.

In 1846 the constitutional convention, tired of the technicality and subtlety of the common-law procedure, required that the procedure should be simplified, and from their requirement came the code of 1849, which, in a simple way, with three hundred and odd sections, introduced a simple procedure that went all over the country as the reform procedure, and which was followed in England — conservative old England — in 1873, by their Adjudicature Act. But now we have been going backwards in this state, and year by year the legislature, whose action was substituted for the old common law, has been adding to the code of procedure, piling up amendment after amendment with specific and particular rules, until we have a code of over three thousand sections, and until every act in a court of justice is regulated by detailed and meticulous statutory provisions; so that when a plain man goes into court, he has to meet at the hands of an acute and ingenious adversary the necessity of litigating upon a great variety of rules which, because they are imposed by the legislature, constitute statutory rights.

He may be right in his claim for justice, and he may be wrong in his practice. Each of these rules is good enough, but all taken together result in a man's finding himself tangled in the form, denied his rights, compelled to litigate until his means are exhausted, so that it is hardly worth his while to go into court. And again, as was done in 1846, as was done in England in 1873, again we need to bring our judicial procedure back to the simple basis of a plain, honest citizen's intelligence.

We have got our procedure regulated according to the trained, refined, subtle, ingenious intellect of the best practiced lawyers, and it is all wrong. Our procedure ought to be based upon the common intelligence of the farmer, the merchant, and the laborer. And there is no reason why it should not be. I say it not without experience in legal procedure. There is no reason why a plain, honest man should not be permitted to go into court and tell his story and have the judge before whom he comes permitted to do justice in that particular case, unhampered by a great variety of statutory rules. And in this convention, acting upon the teaching of the great experience of its members, and following the philosophy of the history of the development of the law, we undertook by plain and adequate provisions to compel the restoration of our judicial procedure to that plain basis of honesty and opportunity.

We found that there had been a vast increase of the expenditures of the state, as well as of the indebtedness of the state; expenditures which had increased from twelve million dollars a year for a number of years after the last convention, to forty-two million dollars a year in the last year. Debts amounting from seven million dollars upwards to one hundred and eighty-six million dollars, amounting to a mortgage for the state and municipal debts, excluding the debt of New York City, of over thirty dollars an acre of the lands of the state, vastly outstripping the increasing population and vastly outstripping the increase in wealth. We found a general belief, clearly with some foundation, that much of the money raised by this enormous increase of debt, had been expended without due return to the people of the state.

Successive administrations of the same party, — administrations of different parties, — all had contributed their part toward this increase of debt; and we looked into the system major importance. That is as true of legislation as it is of administration. But we found that in the legislature the matters of minor detail were retained, and the matters of major importance were receiving scant attention.

The members of the legislature have been going to Albany, each one with his local bill, his private bill, his special bill for some interest in his district, upon the success of which has often depended his reëlection; and the legislature is overwhelmed with a mass of detail, local legislation which ought never to be there at all, and the result of this has been that the legislature has not been adequately discharging its proper function.

Now, we undertook to cure that, and the first thing that we undertook to do was to state the method of dealing with the finances of the state; the method of dealing with the appropriations for the expenses of the state. We found that the legislature was making up the appropriation bills in committee, practically in the dark, suggestions coming from all quarters for what was to go into them, each member of the legislature having something he wanted to get in; and the bills were reported, run along on the calendar, and ordinarily were rushed through in the closing days of the session, with all of the turmoil and uncertainty and doubt as to what was in them, of the all-night sessions.

After the legislature adjourned, the governor had thirty days in which to apply a blue pencil to the work of the legislature and control its action by vetoing the items of the appropriation bills; and so the legislature had abdicated its true function of holding the purse strings; that had been passed over to the governor, and so the legislature was composed of men all of whom were trying to get money out of the state treasury, instead of seeking to protect the state treasury.

Now we undertook to set that right, and we turned the proceeding upside down. It had been standing on its head, and we put it on its feet. We require, in the first place, that the heads of these new departments shall furnish to the governor in adequate time a statement of all the money required by their departments, and that the governor shall then take all these statements, put them together, revise them, prune them, and bring the amounts down to what he is willing to accept responsibility for; and that he is to lay that before the legislature early in its session, together with a statement of the revenues of the state, so that the legislature may have before it at the start a statement of the cloth from which the coat is to be cut, and of the pattern of the coat that is needed.

I undertake to say that every man who tries to keep a cash account finds that it makes him economical. When you sit down and figure your revenue, and put down in another column your necessary expenses, and then see what you have for new things, for optional things, for things you would like, the necessity of condensing your expenditures to meet your revenues makes you economical; and for the first time in the history of our representative government, this constitution requires that process with the finances of the state. For the first time, under that provision, the legislature of the state of New York, having the demands of the executive put before it, and the statement of the revenues out of which those demands are to be met, will be performing its true, traditional function as a representative body, in holding the purse strings, and protecting the purses of the people. Now, you see, that cuts out all these vast assaults upon the treasury by individual members of the legislature, so that they are relieved from the temptation to attend to these local matters instead of attending to the greater interests of the state.

Then we put in a provision prohibiting the passage of bills by the legislature for the expenditure of state money upon local improvements, the building of bridges, culverts, of the press, and they will be the basis of the editorials that are written; and the young man entering the legislature who has the ability to debate the great questions before the legislature for determination, can make his mark; and the legislature instead of being the graveyard of careers, will be an opportunity for political preferment, where ability, and energy, and ambition will enable a man to rise in political life, to show what is in him, to make service in the senate or assembly a stepping-stone to higher public duties.

There are many other things looking in the same direction, which I cannot stop to talk about. These matters are all interrelated; they are all parts of a single whole; they are all the expressions of a desire to bring back to government of the state, its true function; to raise it above the low esteem into which it has fallen; purge it of the habit of playing politics, and to make representative government again its own answer to its detractors, and its own defense against destruction.

Now, we may have been all wrong in the convention. But we were not wrong about the need for something to be done. We were not wrong about the importance to the people of this state, and the people of our country, to have something done to make representative government more effective; and that we were not wrong I can point you to a thousand evidences all over this country of the interest that has been taken in the work of this convention. It seems quite clear to me that all through the West, through the Middle West, and the Mountain West and the Pacific Coast, there has been greater interest taken in this attempt in the state of New York to restore representative government to its true estate than has been taken in the state of New York itself!

There is no mistaking the evidence of private correspondence and the publications of the press all over the country. The people of these states seek and have been discussing the initiative, and the compulsory referendum, and the recall of the administrative officers, and of judges and judicial decisions; they see that in the state of New York we are attempting a great new departure in representative government.

We may have been wrong in the way we devised in the convention to accomplish this, but we were not wrong about the need of it; and as to whether we were wrong about the way, of course, is a question of machinery. I need not tell the members of an economic club of what vast importance the machinery of government is; how important is the question as to whether you have one metal or two for your monetary standard; how important is the question as to whether you issue small notes or not; how important are the questions that are illustrated by the difference between our old National Bank Act and our new National Reserve Act; what vast consequences come under the workings of human nature engaged in business; the conflicting and forward movement of intelligent selfishness on the part of a vast multitude of people; how important are the consequences of all that, under apparently slight differences in machinery. Just so about government. These are matters of governmental machinery. To use a familiar illustration, it is like your automobile when it goes wrong. You do not undertake to cure it by the application of general principles, you do not philosophize about it, or make speeches to it or berate it, or hit it with a club.

You ask somebody who is familiar with machinery, or is intelligent with machinery, to try to put his finger on the little thing that has gone wrong, and as he advances the spark plug, or something else, off it goes.

For five months the men who were elected by the people of the state of New York to overhaul the machinery of government and try to make it go right where it was going wrong, labored with the subject at Albany. They heard everybody who would come; they sent for people who were supposed to know; they heard testimony for weeks and months, and then they discussed it; and they compared their ideas and they adjusted their views. They reconciled their opinions and they brought out their results, and these results are the results which these one hundred and sixty-eight men, after five months' careful study of this machinery, believe will go far to cure the evils that exist in representative government.

The question relative to this constitution is not whether some particular little thing pleases you or me. There is nobody who is wholly satisfied with the constitution. I am not. There are things in it I do not want there. There are things left out, I would like to have there. That was true for every member of the convention. But the great process of free self-government went on; the subordination of minor matters to major matters; the surrendering of individual opinion upon matters of little importance in order to secure agreement upon matters of great importance. That process by which our country is governed and by which free government must always be achieved, went on during those five months, and the result is a great attempt to accomplish something of the first order of importance for our state and country in the form of representative government in a state.

I confess that I thought when the result was reached, that the extraordinary unanimity of the convention upon these great measures, upon this great system composed of these measures, would commend itself to the people of the state. Let me read to you a memorandum which I took from the record, showing you after all the differences of opinion and the long discussion, how the members of all parties in that convention reached their conclusion. There were thirty-three amendments adopted out of over eight hundred. Over eight hundred amendments proposed, and thirty-three adopted; therefore, seven hundred and sixty-seven men against the constitution. These thirty-three were adopted, twelve of them by a unanimous vote; twelve of them by a vote of over ten to one, making twenty-four; of the remaining nine, two were adopted by a vote of over seven to one, two by a vote of over four to one, two by a vote of over three to one, and the remaining three by a vote of over two to one. And of these two are separately submitted — they relate to taxation and apportionment — and the third was one of the minor matters of the convention; I think increase of salaries of legislators. There is another circumstance which emphasizes the extraordinary agreement which resulted from these long discussions. It is that all the great measures of the convention were adopted by a majority, not only of the Republicans, but of the Democrats of the convention.

The Executive Reorganization bill, commonly spoken of as the Short Ballot, was adopted by a vote of Republican ninety-seven to fifteen, Democrat twenty-five to fifteen, total one hundred and twenty-five to thirty, a majority of over four to one.

The budget — that great reform in the financial system of the state; that one bright hope to stop the unbridled waste of public money, which results from a vicious system — was adopted by a vote, Republican one hundred and one to two, Democrat thirty-six to two, a total of one hundred and thirty-seven to four, or more than thirty-four to one.

The City Home Rule provision was adopted by a vote, Republican one hundred and two to two, Democrat eighteen to fifteen, a total of one hundred and twenty to seventeen, or a majority of over seven to one. And let me say that the adverse votes upon that were mainly not against what it did, but as a protest that it did not go farther.

The County Home Rule provision, Republican ninety-one to nine, Democrat thirty-seven to two, total one hundred and twenty-eight to eleven, or a majority of eleven to one.

The Judiciary Article, with its provision for the reform of procedure, Republican one hundred and three to one, Democrat thirty-two to two, total one hundred and thirty-five to three, or a majority of over forty-five to one. When you remember that these two parties, Republican and Democrat, came from long experience in perennial conflict; came from far distant regions in great variety of local conditions; these results of five months of earnest and sincere consideration; these results coming from the true process of self-government certainly do indicate a probability that the provisions adopted will be, in some measure at least, a cure for the evils against which they were devised.

And it seems to me quite clear that no light consideration, no casual glance, would justify any one, any patriotic citizen of the state who wants the evils redressed, in rejecting the conclusions which were reached by that body; I mean with that unanimity, and in that way. If, upon mature considering, it seems to any man that the constitution is wrong, that the things that it seeks ought not to be done, or what it proposes in the way of remedy will be ineffective, or injurious; why, of course, he should vote against it. But, after checking these means to overhaul the machinery of government; and after doing it with this unanimity, I submit to you that no man ought to reject these conclusions, except upon full study and consideration himself, which leads him to a different conclusion.

Of course there is opposition. I have been seeking, I have been wondering much, at the causes. No such series of provisions as this can be adopted without interfering with a great many people. A good many men will be turned out of office. You cannot retrench without turning men out of office. You cannot economize without interfering with people; and if you will look to the opposition to this constitution, in nine cases out of ten you can trace it back to the unwillingness of men to be turned out of office; the fear of men that they will be turned out of office, or the fear of men that their personal perquisites or opportunities will be interfered with.

There is one thing which I feel bound to say: The constitutional convention of 1915 rose above the plane of partisan politics. It rejected, not without struggle, not without a contest, not without strenuous exertions, the desires of some men to use the great majority of the Republican party in that convention, for partisan advantage. It deemed its duty to be to serve the parties to which each man owed allegiance, by serving the state. And that was what led to this extraordinary agreement. That was why Democrats and Republicans alike voted for these great and salutary measures; that was why, after the close of the convention, there was almost unanimous approval of its work by the men engaged in it.

It is with the deepest regret that I observe that among some people, perhaps among many of our fellow-citizens, there is an unwillingness to regard this great and important measure for the public welfare upon the same basis, love of country, and superiority to partisan advantage. All honor to Republicans and Democrats alike who united, regardless of party, to serve their state in seeking to give the people of the state a better government, and regret and sympathy for the future to those who reject that and seek to frustrate this great measure for the public good in order that there may be party advantage gained thereby.

Perhaps I am misled; perhaps I insist unduly upon the work of the convention of which I was part. If I do, you must forgive me. I beg you to do me the honor to believe there is no personal consideration which actuates me. Since I left this city sixteen years ago last summer, to devote myself to the service of the country and the state, I have had but one client. I have had but one desire. I have but one passion: and it has been for the prosperity, and the honor, and the growth in spirit and in power of my country and my state.

I have given out all there was in me into this effort to do what I believed to be necessary for the perpetuity of our free institutions; this effort to make representative government worthy of itself. I have given out my strength, and my life to help bring that about. I hope that it will not prove to have been in vain. No, it cannot have been in vain. This constitution, I believe, will be adopted by the people of the state, but if it is not, the work of the convention will not be lost. It will be but the beginning of a process which, through the working of the processes of free government, will bring out sooner or later, in substance, all the conclusions which are right and sound; for no honest effort in behalf of one's country can ever be lost.

If it be not now that these great measures for reform are adopted, it must be after a hard experience with the evils they are designed to cure. We cannot go on with our government constituted as it is now without suffering for it. For it is bad in system, and we shall come later, if not now, through the lessons of hard experience, to realize that the measures included in this revised constitution are necessary for the well-being of the state and for the continuance of order, liberty, justice, and our free self-government.

GOVERNMENT

ACCEPTANCE OF THE NEW YORK SENATORSHIP

ADDRESS TO THE LEGISLATURE OF NEW YORK
JANUARY 28, 1909

In response to a very wide desire that the state of New York should be represented in the Senate of the United States as its importance required and its traditions demanded, the Republican party of the state honored itself by requesting Mr. Root, then Secretary of State, to accept an election to that body at the hands of the Republican legislature. Upon Mr. Root's expression of a willingness to serve, if elected without any candidacy on his part, the Republican members of the legislature of New York met in caucus and unanimously chose him. Their choice was ratified by the legislature on January 19, 1909. Mr. Root accepted and qualified as senator on March 4, 1909, serving until March 4, 1915.

I HAVE to thank you and I do thank you most sincerely for the very great honor which you have conferred upon me and for the great opportunity that you have set before me — to represent in the Senate of the United States the state of my birth and of my life.

I shall do my best to justify your selection, with not too much confidence in the result, because I do not think that as a rule lawyers who have been many years at the bar and whose habits have become fixed, make very good legislators when they are not caught young, and I have a rather uncomfortable sense that it will be quite impossible for me to live up to the many kindly and delightful things that have been said about me by my friends in the state of New York during the past few months.

I have come to Albany in the hope of meeting the men who are leaders of opinion and of political action in the state of New York and who are, as they ought to be, in the two houses which legislate for the state.

It is my strong desire to get into touch with you as the representatives of the people in the state legislature. I have been for the greater part of the past ten years in Washington, engrossed in the affairs of the national Government which have lain outside even of the limits of the United States, and I feel that I am a little out of touch with the current affairs of the state.

I should like to get back into the same knowledge and familiarity with them that I had years ago when I was here within the state all the time. And I should be glad to establish such a personal relation of acquaintance with every member of the senate and the assembly that if you have anything to say to me as your Senator in Congress you will feel at liberty to do so and that if I have anything to say to you I shall feel at liberty to say it.

I mean this not merely with regard to the filling of offices, although every Senator of the United States is charged with the duty of representing his state in regard to appointments to Federal office from that state and in that state. He is a part of the appointing power, and it is his duty to see that as far as the exercise of his office, in vote and in advice, is concerned, his state has the benefit of its citizens' knowledge of character and reputation in their own communities, so that if a man has lived a good and useful and active life, is respected by his neighbors, is esteemed by them worthy of honor and capable of performing useful public service, this may be made known to the President in Washington through the voice of his representative in the Senate of the United States.

But I mean more than that. Our Government is becoming complicated in a very high degree. Difficult questions are continually presented which affect the interests of every state; and the wide and immense and varied interests of the state of New York are particularly liable to be affected by a great variety of measures which come before the national Congress. I would be glad to have you express your opinions upon all measures which appear to you to affect the interests of the state.

I shall be glad to be at liberty to consult you freely, as occasion offers, upon the practical operation of measures pending before the national Congress.

If you think it will be beneficial to the state of New York, for example, as I now think it would be, to have a parcels post provision included in our postal laws, so that the 39,000 rural free delivery carriers instead of driving around the country with empty buggies, as they do now, shall earn enough to pay their salary by carrying small packages to the people they serve — if you think that would be beneficial to the interests of the state of New York, I shall be glad to have you say so, and if you think I am wrong in that I should be glad to have you say it.

There is more to be considered, however, than the mere interest of the state of New York, in the relation which exists between you and your Senators in Congress. The different states of the Union are no longer isolated communities. They are welded together in their interests, business and social, and the action of every one is felt upon every other. The interests of every one are bound up in the prosperity and the welfare of every other.

With the great and complicated problems which are pressing upon our national Government, it is becoming every year more apparent that the people of no state can live to themselves alone, and that they have set before them as the highest of duties, the obligation to contribute their share to the solving of the great national problems for the maintenance and furtherance of that common interest which is vital to the people of every state but confined by the limits of no state.

Upon these great questions I ask your help in the performance of those duties which you have imposed upon me.

The intimate connection between the people of every locality and of every other state, largely brought about by the increase of communication, the passing to and fro of the trains upon our great railroads, the telegraph and the telephone, the extension of business which knows no state lines, and the substitution of great national centers of business for the old state centers of business, the development of commercial and manufacturing and social life along national lines, has forced upon the national Government the performance of a great variety of duties which formerly were performed by the states within the limits of their comparatively isolated communities.

By the exercise of the powers granted in the interstate commerce clause of the Constitution, the national Government is extending its power over the operation of our railroads, our steamship lines, our telegraph, our express companies. By the exercise of the taxing power it is regulating the action of the people all over the country, as for instance in the Oleomargarine Act. By the exercise still again of the commerce power it is controlling the adulteration of food and deceptive practices in the sale of food, as in the Pure Food law.

The activities of the general Government are continually widening, step by step, covering ground formerly occupied by state action.

That is not a matter of what we wish or what we do not wish; it is not a matter of political program or platform; it is plain fact to be seen by any one and a fact to be considered.

There is one advantage, a great advantage, which has come from it, is coming from it; that is, that we are acquiring effective control over the great developments of business activity in our country in many directions to a degree which could not be possible by state action; that we have growing a strong, virile, competent and effective national Government; that we have built up a great national power respected and honored throughout the world; that America is a name for pride and satisfaction; that from all external attack this powerful national Government protects, and effectively protects, our homes, our families and our lives.

But there are two dangers coming with this same development. One is the danger that the national Government will break down in its machinery through the burden which threatens to be cast upon it. This country is too large, its people are too numerous, its interests are too varied and its activity too great for one central government at Washington to carry the burden of governing all of the country in its local concerns, doing justice to the rights of the individual in every section, because that justice can be done only through intelligent information and consideration.

And the mass of business that is now pressing upon the legislative and executive and judicial branches of our Government in Washington seems to have come about to the limit of their capacity for the transaction of governmental business.

The other danger is the danger of breaking down the local self-government of the states. After all, the thing that we have government for is ultimately the preservation of our homes and our individual liberty. And we ought to be at liberty to regulate the affairs of our homes in accordance with our own ideas.

The tendency to vest all powers in the central government at Washington is likely to produce the decadence of the powers of the states. Now, do not misunderstand me. I am a convinced and uncompromising nationalist of the school of Alexander Hamilton. I believe in the exercise of the executive, the legislative and the judicial powers of the national Government to the full limit of the constitutional grants, as those grants were construed by John Marshall, and would be construed by him today.

But I believe that the founders of the Republic builded more wisely than they knew, when they set the limits between the exercise of that national power and the exercise of the local powers of the states. And while I believe in the exercise of the national power throughout the province of the constitutional grants of national power, I believe also in the preservation of state power within the limits of its constitutional authority.

Further than that, I believe that the essential quality of free government is to be found in the observance by all public officers of the limitations set by law upon their powers. Once admit the right of public officers to disregard limitations upon their powers and you are launched on the course by which good men come to be benevolent despots, with the inevitable corollary that bad men have the opportunity to become tyrannical dictators.

Evidently, if the powers of the states are to be preserved and their authority is to be continued, the states must exercise their powers. The only way to maintain the powers of government is to govern.

Let me say that the men who make the most noise about state rights are very apt to be the men who are the most willing and the most desirous to have the national Government step in and usurp the functions of a state when there is an appropriation carried with the usurpation.

The men who are found opposing the maintenance of the authority of the treaty provisions of the United States made under the express grant of power in the Constitution are apt to be the very men who are anxious to have the Government come into their states and spend no end of money in doing the things that the states ought to do themselves in the exercise of their powers. But the invitation to the national Government to assume this and that duty within the limits of a state is an invitation to set up national power to the ultimate exclusion of state power.

Because I believe in maintaining the two grants of power of the Constitution, maintaining the national power to its full limit and still preserving the state power, I am opposed to everything that tends to belittle, to discredit or to weaken the authority of the legislature of the state.

You cannot take power away from public bodies without having the character of those bodies deteriorate. For this reason I am opposed to the direct election of Senators, as I am opposed to the initiative and referendum, because these things are based upon the idea that the people cannot elect legislatures whom they trust.

They proceed upon the idea of abandoning the attempt to elect trustworthy and competent state legislatures. But if you abandon that attempt, if you begin to legislate or to amend constitutions upon that theory, what becomes of all the other vast powers of the state legislatures, in maintaining the system of local self-government under the Constitution?

If the people of any state are not satisfied to trust their legislature to discharge the constitutional duty of electing senators, let them cure their own faults and elect a legislature that they can trust. Ultimately, in the last analysis, we must come down for successful government to the due performance of the citizens' duty at the polls, and there is no reason to believe that the citizens would perform their duty in the direct election of senators, or in voting upon the initiative or the referendum, any better than they perform it in the election of members of the senates and the assemblies of the states. I am opposed to all steps that proceed upon the theory that the people of our states are to abandon the duty of making their state legislatures able and honored bodies competent to perform the great duties of legislation for those great commonwealths.

Let me say another word which directly bears upon the relations between the performance of your duties and the performance of duties in the body to which you have sent me. The intimate relations between the people who live on one side and the other of different state lines, and the increasing interdependence of people upon each other in wide communities that are not determined by state lines, have created a situation where, in the exercise of a great many of the powers that are reserved in the Constitution to the states, regard ought to be had, not merely to the direct interests of the people within the limits of the states, but also to the claims of neighborhood, the comity that should exist between different communities, the necessity for adjustment of relative rights and interests.

In other words, there is occasion to consider the relations of different states or different communities in different states in the exercise of your powers as well as in the exercise of the national powers.

Take for example the question about the pollution of the harbor of New York, with New York on one side and New Jersey on the other. It is not a subject I have studied, but it is a subject which I observe is up for consideration. I believe suit has been brought by the Attorney-General of the United States regarding it. The states of New York and New Jersey ought to agree upon a reasonable and just solution of the subject without any lawsuit from the Attorney-General of the United States.

There are coming up continually questions in which the legislation of one state will vitally affect the interests of another. Upon those questions it ought not to be necessary for people to press the national Government to come in and usurp the functions of the state in order to have uniformity of treatment on the subject. The states themselves ought to concur, consult, exercise consideration and good neighborhood toward each other in the performance of state functions in matters which affect other states.

The Constitution contemplates such situations, for it provides that states may make agreements with each other by the consent of Congress. It is not necessary that Congress shall stretch and strain its authority, but just in so far as the states neglect to perform their duties in such matters, just so far they invite the pressure upon Congress to lead it to attempt to remedy the evils by stretching the national authority.

We have much to learn. We have much to do. The growing complications and many problems continually presenting themselves and taxing the best thought of the most experienced public servants; the problems of the future, the solutions of which are still undiscovered; the other problems certain to rise that we have not yet discerned — all these are making it more and more vital to the interests of every home in every state that the public servants of the state and the nation shall coöperate in the performance of the functions of government with a spirit of good citizenship, of patriotism and of loyalty to the Constitution under which we live.

To that coöperation jointly with you I pledge myself for the next six years, if I live so long.

THE DIRECT ELECTION OF UNITED STATES SENATORS

ADDRESS IN THE SENATE OF THE UNITED STATES
FEBRUARY 10, 1911

A joint resolution was introduced in the Sixty-first Congress (S. J. Res. 134) to amend the fourth paragraph of Section 2, and the first paragraph of Sections 3 and 4 of Article I of the Constitution of the United States. These paragraphs read as follows:

> Section 2. When vacancies happen in the representation from any State the executive authority thereof shall issue writs of election to fill such vacancies.
>
> Section 3. The Senate of the United States shall be composed of two Senators from each State, chosen by the Legislature thereof, for six years; and each Senator shall have one vote.
>
> Section 4. The times, places, and manner of holding elections for Senators and Representatives shall be prescribed in each State by the Legislature thereof; but the Congress may at any time by law make or alter such regulations except as to the places of choosing Senators.

The joint resolution before the Senate, with the proposed changes in the Constitution indicated in italics, was as follows:

> The Senate of the United States shall be composed of two Senators from each State, *elected by the people thereof* for six years; and each Senator shall have one vote. *The electors in each State shall have the qualifications requisite for electors of the most numerous branch of the State legislatures.*
>
> The times, places, and manner of holding elections for Senators shall be as prescribed in each State by the legislature thereof. [Omits the words: "*but the Congress may at any time by law make or alter such regulations, except as to the places of choosing Senators.*"]
>
> When vacancies happen in the representation *of* any State *in the Senate*, the executive authority *of such State* shall issue writs of election to fill such vacancies: *Provided, That the Legislature of any State may empower the executive thereof to make temporary appointments until the people fill the vacancies by election, as the legislature may direct.*
>
> *This amendment shall not be so construed as to affect the election or term of any Senator chosen before it becomes valid as part of the Constitution.*

The provision to amend Section 4 of Article I to which Mr. Root earnestly objected in his address of February 10, 1911, was rejected by the Senate before the resolution as a whole was voted upon. On February 28, 1911, the joint resolution, as amended, was put to vote and it failed to pass, two-thirds not having voted therefor, the vote being: yeas, 54; nays, 33.

In the Sixty-second Congress, the joint resolution to amend Article I of the Constitution was again introduced (H. J. Res. 39) and passed the House containing the proposed amendment to Section 4 of Article I. In the Senate, Senator Bristow, of Kansas, offered an amendment to the joint resolution which consisted of the omission of the proposed amendment to Section 4 of Article I. Senator Bristow's amendment was adopted and the joint resolution as thus amended, passed the Senate June 12, 1911. The House disagreed to the Senate amendment, and a conference committee was appointed. The conference disagreed, and the Senate insisted upon its amendment. Nearly a year later, on May 13, 1912, the House receded from its disagreement to the Senate amendment, and the joint resolution was then passed without the proposed amendment to Section 4 of Article I. The joint resolution was certified to the Department of State, May 15, 1912, and transmitted to the several state legislatures for action thereon. On May 31, 1913, the Secretary of State, by proclamation, announced that three-fourths of the states (actually 36) having ratified the amendment, it had become valid as the Seventeenth Amendment to the Constitution of the United States.

Mr. Root spoke as follows:

THE joint resolution now before the Senate contains two separate and distinct amendments of the Constitution of the United States. The first amendment proposed is to change the third section of the first article relating to the election of Senators, so that it shall provide for the election of Senators by the people of the several states instead of their election by the legislatures of the states. That is accompanied by an appropriate provision regarding the filling of vacancies which may occur at such time that they cannot conveniently be immediately filled by an election.

The other amendment proposed by the joint resolution is to strike from the fourth section of the first article the provision that —

The times, places, and manner of holding elections for Senators and Representatives shall be prescribed in each state by the legislature thereof; but the Congress may at any time by law make or alter such regulations, except as to the places of choosing Senators.

And to substitute therefor a provision that —

The times, places, and manner of holding elections for Senators shall be as prescribed in each state by the legislature thereof.

That involves two changes in the existing provision. One is to abolish the peremptory command of the Constitution directed to the legislatures of the states, requiring them, as a matter of their duty under the Constitution, to prescribe the times, places, and manner of holding elections for Senators, and to substitute for that peremptory command for the performance of a duty under the Constitution a reference to action which the states may or may not take under their own authority. That change is accomplished by inserting the word " as " in the new provisions. I hope I make it clear.

The present section 4 of the first article of the Constitution provides that —

> The times, places, and manner of holding elections for Senators and Representatives shall be prescribed in each state by the legislature thereof.

That is the command of the nation by the sovereign authority of the Constitution to the legislature of each state, requiring it to prescribe the time, places, and manner of electing Senators; and when they act they act in the execution of a mandate from the nation embodied in the national Constitution. Now read the proposed substitute:

> The times, places, and manner of holding elections for Senators shall be as prescribed in each state by the legislature thereof.

If a state prescribes, well and good. It does it under its own authority. If a state does not prescribe, well and good. There is no mandate of the Constitution of the United States requiring the state to do it. It is a clear, distinct, and unquestionable abandonment of the requirement of the Constitution for this fundamental and essential act under national authority for the preservation of the national life.

The second change in the fourth section of the first article of the Constitution is made by omitting from that section all authority in Congress to make or alter the regulations which are prescribed. The present section reads:

> The times, places, and manner of holding elections for Senators and Representatives shall be prescribed in each state by the legislature thereof; but the Congress may at any time by law make or alter such regulations, except as to the places of choosing Senators.

The proposed substitute for the fourth section reads:

> The times, places, and manner of holding elections for Senators shall be as prescribed in each state by the legislature thereof.

All vestige of national authority as the source of power to perform the act and of national control over the performance of it, or of national power to modify or supplement or compel conformity to national interests, disappears from the provision which is recommended to the Senate in the joint resolution now before us.

Mr. President, I am opposed to both of these amendments. I am opposed to changing the election of Senators from the legislatures to the people at the polls, and I am opposed to abandoning the authority of the National Government over the election and the constitution of the members of this branch of the Government.

Let me first state the reasons why I am opposed to the change in the manner of electing Senators.

It is not wise that the people of the United States should contract the habit of amending the Constitution. Stability in our Government is a matter of vital concern. When America set forth in her great experiment, the almost universal opinion of the world was that she would speedily encounter the disasters that all attempts at popular government had met before that day. The world knew well that the tendency of democratic government was toward frequent change; it knew well that, while all forms of government have weaknesses peculiar to themselves, the weakness of democratic government was its liability to change with the impulse and enthusiasm of the moment, and, through continual changes, to vary from extreme democracy, which men called ochlocracy, on the one hand, to oligarchy and dictatorship on the other. And since the time when our fathers framed the Constitution, half a score of nations, seeking to follow the lines of our experiment, have, in varying degree, and some of them to the last degree of failure, justified such an apprehension.

But with us, Mr. President, there has been one great anchor. In our Constitution we have embodied the eternal principles of justice; we have set up a barrier against ourselves. As Ulysses required his followers to bind him to the mast that he might not yield to the song of the siren as he sailed by, so the American democracy has bound itself to the great rules of right conduct, which are essential to the protection of liberty and justice and property and order, and made it practically impossible that the impulse, the prejudice, the excitement, the frenzy of the moment shall carry our democracy into those excesses which have wrecked all our prototypes in history.

Mr. President, reverence for that great instrument, the belief of mankind in its perpetuity, the unwillingness of our people to tamper with it or to change it, the sentiments that are gathered around it — these, constituting the basis of stability in our Government, are the most valuable of all the possessions of the nation that inhabits this rich and fertile land. Because the American people stand by their Constitution and are unwilling to yield to suggestions that it be tampered with and altered upon slight provocation, every acre of farm-land, every farm-house and barn, every stock of goods, and every manufactory in the country are of greater value. No change in our Constitution should be permitted to cast a doubt upon its permanency and inviolability, unless there be the weightiest and most commanding reasons. All presumptions are against it. The great public policy of a century is against it. A heavy burden rests upon those who wish to make the change.

This is especially true, Mr. President, when a change is proposed which in any degree alters the delicate relations which exist between the national and the state governments, or which in any degree affects or modifies any of those great compromises of the Constitution which enabled the thirteen original colonies, different in interests, in traditions, in size, in population, and in industries, to adjust their different views and to enter into a binding agreement.

Whenever a proposal is made to change the provisions that affect the relations between the states and the National Government, or to modify any of the terms of one of those great compromises upon which the institution rests, there are special reasons for rejecting it, and a double burden rests upon those who propose it. For more than one hundred years the provisions of this instrument as they are, with every sentence weighed, with every word scanned and receiving its full meaning, have been considered and clarified and determined upon by the courts. Our people have become accustomed to statutes based upon these provisions as they are. A great war has been fought to settle the most vital and important of the questions arising under this instrument as it is. The different parts have become adjusted to each other. We have come to understand what their relation is. The ship has found itself and we are free, after a century of discussion, from serious questions as to the relations of the general and state governments.

How the field of discussion has changed! Look at the old records of Congress, and you will find them filled with animated and excited controversies which have passed away. And now I say that for us to launch into a new era of changed provisions and new questions arising from them, would be justified only by the most serious and weighty reasons. Changes by amendment may seem to gentlemen who propose them simple, and their effect may seem to be unquestionable. But, Mr. President, no one can foresee the far-reaching effect of changing the language of the Constitution in any manner which affects the relations of the states to the general government. How little we know what any amendment would produce!

One hundred and seven years ago we made an amendment relating to the election of the President and Vice-President. Has that amendment produced the result which its authors expected? No; far from it. The results of action under that amendment are as different from those which were expected by its authors as our Government is different from the government of any Oriental power.

Forty-five years ago we made a series of amendments, following upon the great Civil War. Have those amendments worked out as their authors expected? No. No man can open to the fourteenth and fifteenth amendments of the Constitution, and for a moment maintain that they have accomplished what the Congress of the United States expected them to accomplish when it passed the resolutions for their submission, or what the state legislatures expected when they approved them.

We enter upon a field of doubt, of new discussions, the end of which no man can foresee, when we begin to tamper with the delicately adjusted machinery to which we have been so long accustomed and which we now understand so well.

Mr. President, there has been but little attempt here to assign reasons for the proposed change in the election of Senators. It has been left in the main to rest upon the proposition that the people of the country desire it; that there have been resolutions adopted by many legislatures; that planks have been put in many political platforms; and that as a whole the people of the country wish for the change.

I am convinced, sir, and I think I can anticipate a general agreement from the members of this chamber in the proposition, that the desire of the people for this change, if there be a desire, is not a very active and violent feeling. It is a rather mild assent to a proposition which is suggested to them as an appropriate remedy for certain ascertained and recognized evils. There is, we all know, a general tendency in all democracies to favor propositions which look to the extension of power at the polls. Extension of suffrage, extension of the direct power of the voters at the polls, naturally receive assent at first blush.

There is another tendency which is natural and in which we all share, and that is that when an evil is recognized, and some one suggests that such and such a provision of law will cure the evil, our interest is attracted and our support is conciliated for the proposed measure.

I submit that what the people of the country really want is to have certain evils which they recognize in the present election of Senators cured, and that they are quite indifferent about this change except as it is certified to them to be a sure cure for the evils. Whether it will be a cure or not has been little discussed and little considered by the people of the United States, and it has been little discussed and little considered by the Senate.

The evil which the people of the country wish to see cured, and which I wish to see cured with them, and we all do, consists of certain patent defects in the working of the system of election of Senators by the state legislatures.

The first of those is a defect in the execution of the law which requires them to select. It is the deadlock that exists so frequently. The inexplicable delay of the legislature of Montana to return my friend, the Senator from Montana [Mr. Carter], the obstinacy of all branches of the Democratic party in the legislature of New York, the reluctance of the legislature of Iowa to follow any of its great and gifted leaders, all these cause dissatisfaction on the part of the people, and, I believe, constitute the chief reason for the assent of the people to propositions to change the manner of election.

But, Mr. President, is it not our duty to say to the people of the United States that these deadlocks come not from the constitutional provision, that they come from our statute of 1866? They can be ended forever on any day by this Congress through a simple amendment of the statute. For the deadlocks arise from the fact that our statute requires a majority vote, and everywhere among people of independence and individual will it is a difficult thing to secure a majority vote.

If we chose today to amend our statute so that the legislatures of these states could elect by a plurality, they would elect tomorrow. If we chose to say that in any legislature where a majority vote should not be obtained within thirty days of the beginning of the Congress in which the successful candidate was to take his seat, there should be an election by plurality, in every one there would be an election the day after the period expired. And what is more, there would be majorities obtained in order to avoid those elections by pluralities.

But we have not chosen to do it. We have fallen upon times when it seems as if not the last thing, but the first thing that is to be done to cure an evil, is to amend the Constitution of the United States. Mr. President, this very joint resolution proposing to amend the Constitution of the United States will force us to abandon the majority rule and to entrust the election of Senators to a plurality, for never can the Senate of the United States maintain a working force if a majority vote is required for the election of Senators by the people of the several states.

I appeal to a universal recognition of the fact that it will not be practicable to have Senators elected under a requirement of a majority vote in case this amendment to the Constitution is adopted. In every close state, the outlying parties, the irreconcilables, not occasionally or accidentally, but as a rule, poll more votes than the difference between the two great parties, and that means that, as a rule, in the close states of the Union, no one is elected by a majority vote.

So, sir, we are proposing to cure this evil by an amendment of the Constitution which lands us in the same position as to the rule of majority or plurality that we would reach if we cured it as we can cure it absolutely, by an amendment of our statute.

But there is another reason why the people are dissatisfied with the discharge of the functions of our state legislatures. From time to time there are rumors, suspicions, and occasionally proofs of corrupt conduct on the part of state legislatures, and from time to time a belief that state legislatures have been influenced by personal considerations or controlled by extra-official influences in the performance of their duty.

Mr. President, we are too apt, in having our attention fixed upon the exceptional, to forget the usual. It is true that what have long been known in this chamber as forbidden and abhorrent forces do sometimes affect the election of a Senator; but it is only occasional, and the great body of the members of the Senate are, and always have been, elected as the free and intelligent judgment of their state legislatures dictate.

There is no claim, sir, that I have heard, certainly there has been no ground suggested to sustain a claim, that an honest and intelligent legislature, fairly canvassing the abilities and the character of the men who can best serve their country as Senators for their states, cannot make as good a choice, if not a better choice, than the electorate at large.

There has been no claim, or certainly no ground stated to sustain a claim, that the wise men who framed our Constitution were mistaken in their belief that wise and intelligent and faithful state legislatures would make the best possible choice for Senators of the United States.

No; the real ground is that, arguing from these exceptional and occasional cases, the people of the United States have been led to believe that the legislatures of their states are unfaithful to their trust in making their selections, and that they will continue unfaithful.

Mr. President, what is the remedy the people of the United States should seek, if this be true? Are they to abandon the performance of their duty in the election of their state legislatures? Are they to abandon the system, rather than reform the system? This whole proposition rests upon the postulate of the incapacity of the people of the United States to elect honest and faithful legislatures. If the framers of the resolution had made it read so that it would express the true principle on which they base it, they would have made it read like this:

> WHEREAS, The people of the several states have proved incompetent to select honest and faithful legislators in their own states:
>
> *Resolved*, That the Constitution of the United States be so amended as to relieve the people from the consequences of their incompetency by taking from the state legislatures the power to choose Senators of the United States and vesting that power in the same incompetent hands.

But, Mr. President, if the people of our states are to abandon the attempt and be faithless to the duty to elect honest and faithful legislatures, what becomes of the governments of our states? In the growing complication of life, the daily increasing interdependence of all men under our highly developed social system, under which for food, for clothing, for shelter, for fuel, for health, for opportunities for business and for transportation, at every side and on every occasion in life we are dependent on each other, day by day we grow to rely more and more on the government that is regulating all the agencies that are necessary to our lives. What government shall perform that function? If the state government is abandoned, if we recognize the fact that we cannot have honest legislatures, sir, the tide that now sets toward the Federal Government will swell in volume and in power. Here is a power that can answer the demands of life.

Let me tell the gentlemen who are solicitous for the preservation of the sovereignty of their states, that there is but one way in which they can preserve that sovereignty, and that is by repudiating absolutely and forever the fundamental doctrine upon which this resolution proceeds. Let them go home to their states when this session ends and invoke the patriotism of their people to make the government of their states worthy of the great duties that rest upon them and competent to preserve the autonomy of their states against that incursion of Federal power which is being continually urged, urged, urged, by those who fail to find satisfaction from the governments of the states.

In my humble judgment, sir, the most vital thing to be done in the United States today is to strengthen the legislatures of the states. I fear the breaking down of the government of the United States by the accumulation of demands upon it, through the gradual weakening of the state governments, through the failure of the state governments to keep pace with the continually increasing demands of our social and business life.

We have come very near the limit, sir, of what we can competently do, very near the limit of what we can do as well as it ought to be done. Our executive officers are overburdened. The business of this Congress is conducted with less and less knowledge on the part of the members of the body in general as to what the committees have been doing. We are forced session by session to more complete reliance upon the reports of the committees, with less and less consideration from the members of the Congress at large. Our judicial force is being overburdened and our calendars clogged, and we are looking about for ways to relieve this court and that from too heavy a burden, and to prevent the law's delays.

Let us continue upon the theory that state governments are corrupt and incompetent. The time will come when the

Government of the United States will be driven to the exercise of more arbitrary and unconsidered power, will be driven to greater concentration, will be driven to extend its functions into the internal affairs of the states; and then sooner or later the people of the country will reject a government that has subjected their personal and intimate neighborhood affairs to the control of a central power in Washington, and then, in the place of competent states governing their own affairs, we shall go through the cycle of concentration of power at the center while the states dwindle into insignificance, and ultimately the breaking up of the great Republic upon new lines of separation.

Mr. President, there is another view of the fundamental proposition on which this resolution rests. It is an expression of distrust for representative government. It does not stand alone. It is a part of the great movement which has been going on now in these recent years throughout the country, and in which our people have been drifting away from their trust in representative government. These modern constitutions which are filled with specific provisions, limiting and directing the legislature in every direction, furnishing such startling contrasts to the simplicity of the Constitution of the United States, are an expression of distrust in representative government. The "initiative" is an expression of distrust in representative government. The "referendum" is an expression of distrust in representative government.

This resolution is an expression of the same sentiment. And strangely, sir, this movement comes at the very time when the development of our country in its business and social and political life makes it all the more necessary that we should depend upon representative government. We have gone far, far away from the days of the old New England town meetings. I doubt if some of the Senators coming from states of small population realize how far we have gone in the great industrial communities of the East and the Middle West from that condition in which direct democratic government is possible.

Mr. President, this whole series of expressions of distrust, the detailed limiting constitutions, the initiative, the referendum, the amendment of the Constitution which is now before us, are all an expression of that weakness of democracies which it is the function of the Constitution to guard democracies themselves against.

Mr. President, what is to become of the state legislatures if we follow the principles of this resolution? If you rob them of power, of dignity, of consequence, what will be the personnel of the state legislatures? We have had illustrations. The boards of aldermen in some of our American cities, originally bodies of high consideration, filled by citizens of consequence and of high standing among their fellows, have dwindled and sunk to insignificance and worthlessness, as power after power has been taken away from them. Once begin the progress in that direction by taking the first step based upon the principle of this resolution and you will find the members of our state legislatures growing less and less competent, less and less worthy of trust, and less and less efficient in the performance of their duties.

You can never develop competent and trusted bodies of public servants by expressing distrust of them, by taking power away from them, by holding them up to the world as being unworthy of confidence. Honest men, good men, self-respecting men, men whose standing in their community makes it desirable for the public service that they shall go into our state legislatures, will never subject themselves to be ranked in bodies suspected and discredited and deprived of power.

Mr. President, this resolution providing for an amendment is not an expression of confidence in the people; it is an expression of distrust in the people. It is not progress; it is a slipping back. It is not an improvement on our system of government; it is an abandonment of our system of government.

The true remedy for the evils that we see is not to abandon our duty, but to perform it. Sir, there is no weaker course for men to take than to endeavor to make up for the failure to do their duty by changing the form of the duty. This is a proposition that the people of the several states who have stayed away from the polls, who have been deaf to the considerations of public interest, who have allowed personal favoritism to supplant their desire to select the best public servants, who have been bought to cast their franchises, as the people of Adams County, Ohio, were bought, instead of curing themselves and performing their duty in the election of their state legislatures, shall try another way to select Senators of the United States. It is a proposition that the people who cannot elect honest men from their own neighbors can elect honest men to the Senate of the United States.

Sir, what vote ever cast by an American citizen can be cast with a stronger probability that it is well informed than a vote for a member of his legislature? He is a neighbor; he is a man whom he has known all his life; he knows all about him. How can the men who are unable or unwilling to perform the duty of making a selection of an honest and faithful legislator from their own vicinage improve upon their performance in the selection of a candidate in a statewide election of candidates whom most of them know very little or nothing about, except what they get from the newspapers?

Sir, apart from that, it is never possible to cure neglect of duty by changing the form. There is but one safety for a popular government. No matter what constitutions you have or what statutes you enact, sooner or later you come to the polls; and if you do not have virtue and public spirit there, your government goes down.

I press upon the Senate now the duty of saying that it will not give its assent to any attempt at an evasion of that duty by the people of the United States. The pathway lies clear before them under the Constitution. If they will do their duty, the Constitution needs no amendment. If they do not do their duty, you can amend the Constitution a thousand times without any utility. Here, if anywhere, the truth ought to be told; here, if anywhere, should be found men with the courage to say to their own constituents: "The trouble in the election of Senators of the United States is not in the Constitution; it is with you; it is because you are not doing your duty." If there be no voice found in this land with authority and power to reach the minds of our people with such a message, then we are caucusing over idle words when we talk of an amendment to the Constitution.

Mr. President, it is wholly unnecessary to abandon the attempt to elect honest legislatures. The whole purpose of relieving and remedying the evil which has led to this agitation for an amendment to the Constitution can be accomplished, and it is in process of being accomplished, without an amendment. We are today in a condition of affairs political, social, and business which is but temporary. The enormous increase in the productive capacity of mankind, followed by an enormous increase of wealth, an increase which always in the beginning is congested before the processes of distribution are fully at work, is in active operation. The necessity for a readjustment of the relations of government to the great properties that constitute and continually create wealth, to the great enterprises through which that wealth is gained and is continued — the necessity for a readjustment of the relations of government to these new conditions has led to a control over our state legislatures in many cases which is abnormal, which is to be condemned, and which has been the cause of practically and substantially all the evils that underlie the desire for a reform. That control has been exercised in part through a form of political organization which grew up under simpler conditions and is in many respects outgrown by our people, and in part by the direct application of the wealth which was seeking to save itself from destruction in the readjustment of conditions to influence the action of legislators.

I say that condition is temporary. I say the process of relieving it is going on, and is going on all over this land. I think it has been proceeding longer in the Southern states and then in the Western states, and now in the Eastern states. With many of the expedients for the readjustment I do not agree; with many of them I do agree. Of this I am certain, that, altogether, they exhibit the strivings of a great democracy adjusting itself to new conditions, and they are bound to result in a successful accomplishment. The pendulum will swing to and fro. Experiments will be tried and abandoned. Experiments will be tried and found successful here, and needing modification there; but ultimately we shall come back to a new adjustment under the new relations, having all the competency of popular government that existed before the great increase of wealth in our generation.

Mr. President, the proposers of this joint resolution ask that we shall make one of the first steps in this great experimental process, the irrevocable step, of amending the Constitution of the United States. Ah, Mr. President, that is an inconsiderate proposal. It is hardly worthy of grave and experienced legislators. The time may come, after all these experiments have been worked out, when it will be found necessary to amend the Constitution. I do not believe it will; I am confident that under the broad terms of that instrument, which has been sufficient for all the growth and change of a century and a quarter, the process of reform which has now begun, will go on to a successful end, in conformity to the Constitution as it is. But, if I am wrong, if at some time or other it becomes needful to amend the Constitution for the purpose of remedying evils, let us amend it after the experiment, and not at the beginning; let us do it as the result of that experience which brings wisdom, and not as the result of those conjectures which lead to continual change.

Mr. President, there are specific reasons against this change. The first and great reason in my mind is that it is inconsistent with the fundamental design of the Senate. The purpose of the Constitution was to create in the Senate a body which would be as unlike as possible to the other House. It was to be a body more secure in tenure, different in the manner of its election, different in its responsibility, more conservative, more deliberate than the other House, which responds year by year to every movement of the public mind and the public feeling. As the limitations of the Constitution were set up by the American democracy to protect them against themselves in every impulse to violate the fundamental rules of justice, so the Senate was established by the Constitution to protect the American democracy against itself in the legislation which was required under the Constitution.

The framers of the Constitution realized that the weakness of democracy is the liability to continual change; they realized that there needed to be some guardian of the sober second thought; and so they created the Senate to fulfill that high and vitally important duty. Mr. President, this change tends to decrease the difference between the Senate and the lower House. It tends to make the two more alike; it tends to make the function of the Senate less distinctive, and to reduce the benefit which the Senate can render to the public service.

Government over the elections in the state or whether the resolution proposed by the committee provides for taking away an existing power.

Let me state what I think it is. As the Constitution now stands, Senators are elected by legislatures whose proceedings are under the control and regulation of the national Congress. The resolution proposes to transfer the power of election from the legislatures to the popular electorate without extending to the new electorate that power of national control. The Sutherland amendment proposes to carry over to the new body of electors the same control which the present Constitution attaches to the existing power of electors.

Now, Mr. President, we are told that that is too high a price for the South to pay. The Senator from Mississippi [Mr. Percy] has said to us:

> Notwithstanding the suggestions of the Senators from New York and Montana, the day may be far distant, if it will ever come, when any political party will again find it expedient to attempt to enact Federal laws for the supervision of elections. But this optimistic hope furnishes no safe reason for extending the power of the Government as to the enactment of such laws, and I would not be dealing in frankness with our Republican allies, who are supporting us in this measure, and for whose patriotism and earnestness in the support of it I have the profoundest respect, if I did not say to them that in my judgment the extension of the power of the Federal Government, as required by the Sutherland amendment, is a price greater than the South is willing to pay for the election of Senators by the direct vote of the people. I have no hesitancy in saying that it is a price greater than it should pay.

Mr. President, I beg leave to say to the Senator from Mississippi and to his Republican allies, from a heart full of sympathy with all measures of conciliation between the two parts of the country, that the time has not yet come when the people of this nation are entering the market-place to buy from them or from any of them the right to preserve and protect by the exercise of our own national power the Government of the United States under its Constitution.

of the Government of the United States over the process of constituting its own legislative body, in order to secure the change of election from a state legislature to the people of the several states. It is a new, additional, independent, disconnected, and unnecessary amendment to the Constitution. It has no place in the deliberations of this body or of any body upon the change in the manner of electing Senators. A change from the election by the legislature to an election by the people can be made with or without the other amendment, and wholly unaffected by it.

The people of the United States may wish for one and may not wish for the other. They ought not to be compelled to vote for one, which they may not wish for, as a condition of securing the other, which they may wish for. Each should stand upon its own basis. The people of the country should have an opportunity to vote to change the manner of the election of Senators, if they wish for it, without being compelled, as the price of getting it, to vote for the destruction of that control which the National Government has had from the beginning over the constitution of this great branch of the national institution.

I believe that the adoption of this amendment to section 4, which takes away the power of Congress to make in the last resort, if it finds it necessary, regulations to secure the effective, the honest, the uncontrolled selections of members of the Senate, would be a reversal of the theory of the Constitution. I believe that it would strike a blow at that power of independent self-support which is essential to the perpetuity and the effectiveness of government. I believe that it would be a reversion to the theory of the old confederation, under which the Government of the United States was dependent upon the states, and an abandonment of the theory of the Constitution under which we live, which was that the Government of the United States should stand erect and self-sustaining and have all the powers necessary for the maintenance of national life, dependent upon no state, upon no state legislature, and upon no power whatever except the power of the nation itself. . . .

We have had occasion to exercise the power of regulation both in regard to the election of members of the House of Representatives and in regard to the election of Senators. Congress in 1842 passed a statute to regulate the election of members of the House. It was found necessary in order to have effective and proper elections. It has passed repeated statutes since then, notably in 1872, and our elections are being conducted now under those statutes passed by the Congress. Congress has found occasion to regulate the election of Senators, and those elections are being conducted now under the statute passed in 1866. No man can say that the time will not come again when it will be necessary for the Congress, in order to secure uniformity, in order to secure effectiveness, in order to prevent abuses, to exercise its power in respect of regulating the times and the manner of electing members to each House of the national legislature.

But it was not my purpose, as I have already stated, to re-argue this case. I have stated the substantial grounds upon which I prefer that the substitute offered by the Senator from Kansas shall take the place of the original joint resolution. I shall oppose the resolution, then, on the ground that I think it is inexpedient and unnecessary to make any amendment of the Constitution at all in regard to the election of Senators. I believe that it will result in a deterioration of the personnel of the Senate. I believe that it will keep out of the Senate a large and important element well adapted to the performance of the peculiar and special duty of the Senate in our system of government. I believe that all the abuses which have led to such a desire for this change on the part of the people of the country can be cured by a simple amendment of the law, by amending the statute rather than by amending the Constitution of the United States.

Such a step I have already introduced. It was introduced at the last session and favorably reported by the Committee on Privileges and Elections. It has been introduced again at this session and is now pending before the Committee on Privileges and Elections. It provides for the election of Senators by a plurality, which is something that would be inevitable if we transfer the right of election from the legislatures to the people. It cures the evils which we have had by a simple amendment of the law. It affords an opportunity for a majority rule to control for a period which is stated in the bill as introduced at twenty days, after the first convening of the two houses of the legislature. After the operation of twenty days has failed to produce an election by the majority rule, it provides for the application of a plurality rule.

I fully recognize the fact that we have going on throughout a large part of the country a process of change, a process of experiment in the way of modifying our governmental institutions. I recognize the fact that the people of many states have become dissatisfied with the way in which their political machinery has acted and that they desire to change it. I have great sympathy with the feeling and take great interest in the experiments that are being tried. I believe that good will come from the awakened interest of the people of the country in their own political affairs and from their determination to take a part in their affairs and to make their will effective.

But it is a process of experiment. We cannot change the institutions of more than a century without long trial and consideration. Experiments will fail; experiments will not succeed. All of us will see opportunities for modification and improvement. No one of us can evolve from his own thought, not all of us together can by conference produce results which we may feel sure are better than the methods devised by the framers of our Government, until the results have been put to the test of practical application.

The system under which we live has produced the best results that ever have come from the experiments of mankind in government. We have received from our present institutions manifold blessings, and in the providence of God have wrought out under those institutions results which have made for the happiness, for the liberty, for the advancement of all mankind. With all history strewn with the wrecks of government, with human nature still unchanged, I would hesitate long before assuming that my own judgment, or the judgment of all of us, can improve the system and framework of our Government, except upon experiment and demonstration by practical application.

I do not like to see experiments begin or proceed in their early stages by amendments to the Constitution in advance of their being tried out fully. Amendments should be the result of long deliberation and trial. They should not initiate deliberation and trial.

For these reasons, I shall take the course regarding the substitute and the joint resolution which I have indicated, whether the substitute be adopted or not.

THE CASE OF SENATOR LORIMER

ADDRESS IN THE SENATE OF THE UNITED STATES
FEBRUARY 3, 1911

William Lorimer, of Illinois, after serving seven terms in the House of Representatives, was elected United States Senator from Illinois by the legislature of that state, May 26, 1909, for the term 1909–1915.

Mr. Lorimer took his seat June 18, 1909, and on June 20, 1910, the Senate passed a resolution authorizing and directing the Committee on Privileges and Elections to investigate his election. This Committee reported December 21, 1910, to the effect that his election had not been invalidated by corrupt practices, and a minority report was submitted January 9, 1911.

While these reports were under discussion, Mr. Root made the address which follows.

On March 1, 1911, a resolution declaring Mr. Lorimer's election invalid was defeated by a vote of 40 to 46. On June 2, 1911, the Senate passed a resolution appointing a special committee to investigate again the Lorimer case. The majority of this special committee reported in favor of Mr. Lorimer, May 20, 1912, and on July 13, 1912, a resolution of the minority that corrupt methods and practices had rendered Mr. Lorimer's election invalid, was adopted by the Senate by a vote of 55 to 28.

ON the twentieth of June last the Senate passed a resolution which directed the Committee on Privileges and Elections —

to investigate certain charges against William Lorimer, a Senator from the state of Illinois, and to report to the Senate whether in the election of said William Lorimer as a Senator of the United States from said state of Illinois there were used or employed corrupt methods or practices.

The Committee on Privileges and Elections have now reported, not whether there were used or employed corrupt methods or practices in the election of William Lorimer, but that, in their opinion, the title of Mr. Lorimer to his seat in the Senate has not been shown to be invalid by the use or employment of corrupt methods or practices; and the committee request to be discharged from further consideration of the resolution.

It is a fair inference, from a comparison between the terms of the resolution and the report of the committee, that the committee were of the opinion that there were corrupt practices used and employed in the election of Mr. Lorimer, but that the legal effect of such corrupt methods and practices was not such as to invalidate his election. That view of the true meaning of the committee's report is supported by an examination of the testimony which was before them.

I am constrained, upon a careful examination of the testimony, to disagree with the conclusions of the committee. I do it with great regret; I do it unwillingly, because I have the highest respect for the members of the committee and for their judgment. I know that they are trained and able men and that they are men of the purest patriotism and of a character which makes it impossible even to discuss the integrity of their action. It is difficult for me to reconcile myself to taking a different view of the facts in this case from that which these trusted and honored colleagues have taken after hearing the witnesses; and, Mr. President, I differ from them with great regret, because the conclusion which I have reached involves the interest, and, if agreed to by the Senate involves the injury, of a gentleman toward whom I have the kindliest feelings, Mr. Lorimer; involves a disgrace to the great state of Illinois and to the country of which that state is so great and potent a part. But I cannot come to any different conclusion.

I differ from the committee, sir, not only as to their conclusion, but as to the view of the scope and nature of their duties, which I believe played a considerable part in leading them to their conclusion.

The charges against Mr. Lorimer were presented to the committee by counsel for the *Chicago Tribune*. The committee deemed it to be their duty to treat the charges from the beginning to the end as they would have treated a private complaint against a private defendant, holding the complainant to strict proof as a court would have held a private litigant, and the committee concluded that the charges had not been sustained.

It is true, as the Senator from Texas [Mr. Bailey] said upon this floor a few days ago, that the wisdom of ages has shown that the best way to get at the truth of a case is to have two parties and to hear their testimony and their arguments; but, Mr. President, who has made the *Chicago Tribune* a party to an investigation of a question that concerns the integrity, the purity, the reputation, and the authority of the Senate of the United States? When have we committed to that newspaper, or to any newspaper, to the owners of a paper and their counsel, or to any man, the guardianship of our honor and the preservation of the integrity of our Government? No, Mr. President, when it once appeared to the committee that there was substantial ground for the charges, when one witness had appeared before them and given testimony which, if believed, established the fact of bribery, then from that time, I submit to the Senate, it became the duty of the Committee on Privileges and Elections to do what the Senate resolution directed them to do — to investigate the charges and to report to the Senate, not whether the *Chicago Tribune* had established a case, but whether in the election there were used or employed corrupt methods or practices.

And, Mr. President, the case is full of opportunities of which a different view would have led the committee undoubtedly to avail themselves to secure fuller and more satisfactory information upon the subject of the resolution. The evidence taken points clearly to avenue after avenue which could be followed down to probable information upon the subject of the resolution; but, in taking the view of their duty which they did, the committee logically and naturally excluded much information which was brought forth by questions put to witnesses, and which would naturally have opened opportunity for further information.

The framework of the events to which the investigation related is familiar to all the members of the Senate. From January until May 26, 1909, the legislature of Illinois was engaged in fruitlessly balloting for a Senator to succeed Mr. Hopkins, who was then a member of the Senate.

Mr. Hopkins had received a large vote by way of instruction in the primaries, and Mr. Stringer was the primary selection of the Democratic party, and the votes ran for many weeks, for months, with the greater part of the Republicans voting for Mr. Hopkins, but a sufficient number of votes scattering about to prevent an election, and the greater part of the Democrats voting for Mr. Stringer.

On the twenty-sixth of May there was a sudden change, and the votes of a very large part of the Republicans and of the Democrats were turned to Mr. Lorimer, who up to that time had not been an avowed candidate, only an occasional scattering vote having been cast for him. On that day there were two hundred and two members of the legislature of Illinois present in the joint session of the two houses, making one hundred and two votes necessary to an election. On the ballot to which I have referred, on the roll-call of the senate, there were ten votes for Mr. Lorimer, and on the roll-call of the house there were ninety-one for Mr. Lorimer, making a total of one hundred and one votes. Thereupon seven Republican senators who had voted for Mr. Hopkins on the roll-call changed their votes from Mr. Hopkins to Mr. Lorimer, making one hundred and eight votes for Mr. Lorimer, and he was declared to be elected. Those one hundred and eight votes were fifty-three of them cast by Democrats and fifty-five by Republicans.

The investigation concerns itself with the way in which those one hundred and eight votes were procured. It is practically concentrated upon the way in which the fifty-three Democratic votes were secured, because it was a matter for special inquiry that fifty-three Democrats should leave the candidate of their own primary and unite upon a candidate of the opposite party.

Now, there are certain undisputed facts which bear upon this inquiry as to these fifty-three Democratic votes. The first which I ask you to consider is that Mr. Lorimer was present at Springfield and in attendance at the state capital at the time of this election, and he had been there for several weeks. It appears that one of the Democrats who had been asked to vote for Mr. Lorimer raised some objection and was requested to go into the Speaker's room — this is on the day of the election — and see Mr. Lorimer.

He had asked for certain promises regarding patronage, regarding the appointment of Federal officers in his own town. He was requested to go, and he did go into the Speaker's room, and there found Mr. Lorimer; and he had with Mr. Lorimer a conversation relating to the appointment of Federal officers in his town, and it appeared to be satisfactory.

Mr. Lorimer then was present in the capitol, occupying the room of the Speaker of the assembly, and there meeting and having interviews with the members of the assembly regarding their voting for him.

The second important fact bearing upon the relation between Mr. Lorimer's election and these Democratic votes is that the agent selected by Mr. Lorimer, the chief agent to secure Democratic votes for him, was Mr. Lee O'Neil Browne. Mr. Browne was the leader of one faction of the Democrats in the assembly. There were two factions, each with a leader. Mr. Browne had between thirty and forty, and another, Mr. Tippet, had between twenty and thirty Democratic members of the legislature, and Mr. Browne was called into consultation, conference, coöperation with Mr. Lorimer and became plainly Mr. Lorimer's accredited and authorized agent in securing votes from the Democratic side of the assembly.

This rests upon the testimony of Mr. Browne himself, and is not subject to any dispute. Mr. Browne says, after being asked about whether he had reported some facts to Mr. Lorimer:

A. Well, now, if I was giving you my best judgment as to when I first spoke to Senator Lorimer personally about the matter, I would say it was somewhere in the neighborhood of a week.

Q. A week? — A. Somewhere.

Q. What — and then you conferred with him frequently, did you not? — A. Oh, yes.

Q. Every day? — A. I presume every night. The conferences were at night mostly. Every night during the stay in Springfield.

Q. Yes. And those conferences lasted some hours, didn't they? — A. Sometimes they did, and sometimes there were a dozen of them in an evening.

Q. And you kept Senator Lorimer posted as to your movements with reference to his candidacy, did you? — A. We all kept each other posted, just as any other campaign committee would do.

Q. Well, I am asking you whether you kept him posted as to your movements with reference to his candidacy? — A. I have answered that.

Q. Well, did you keep him posted? — A. We all kept each other posted.

Q. What I want to know is, did you tell Mr. Lorimer, the candidate for United States Senator, as to what you were doing toward furthering his candidacy? — A. I presume I did.

It further appears that Mr. Browne had made a condition of bringing his followers to the support of Mr. Lorimer, that none of them should be expected to vote for Mr. Lorimer until there was satisfactory assurance that the votes would be sufficient to elect. Mr. Browne says:

Q. So you insisted that no Democrat should vote for Mr. Lorimer until you were advised that there should be enough votes, outside of the Democrats, with them, to elect him? — A. Well, I insisted, and I made it a matter of honor, with both of them —

Mr. Lorimer and Mr. Shurtleff —

that no roll-call for Mr. Lorimer's election should be started, and that I would not consent to a single one of my followers voting for him until I became sure that there were enough with those to elect him.

He is asked now:

Q. Now, what did you do, if anything, to notify the men who belonged to your faction, who you believed would vote for Mr. Lorimer, that the vote would be taken on the twenty-sixth ? — A. Well, I cannot say to you, Senator, just what course I pursued with every one of them. I know the message was carried in one way or another to each one of them that the roll-call would be put on the next day for his election, and that it was going to go through.

Q. You set in motion some machinery by which all of your friends who you believed would vote for Mr. Lorimer — I believe you said thirty — were notified that it would be called off on that day, so that all of them would be on hand, and it would be called off on that day, the twenty-sixth ? — A. Well, all of them were on hand those days all of the time, Senator.

Q. You notified them that the ballot would be taken on that day ? — A. Yes.

Q. Or had it done ? —A. Yes.

Q. So that they might be present ? — A. Yes.

I say the testimony, undisputed and unquestionable, leaves no doubt of the relation of agency between Mr. Browne and Mr. Lorimer in the securing of the Democratic votes, or at all events the thirty Democratic votes cast by followers of Mr. Browne and constituting a part of the one hundred and eight votes that elected Mr. Lorimer.

The relation of Mr. Browne as leader of these thirty voters is very well shown by his own testimony, which I will now read:

Q. As minority leader, I suppose your vote would be taken as a criterion on strictly party questions, to those who should follow you, as to party policy in voting ? — A. Well, in this transaction I might say the bellwether, so to speak, was Manny Abrahams — Emanuel Abrahams. He is the first on the list, you will see, the first Democrat; and he was a very strong and stanch adherent of mine, and, whether right or wrong, he believed what I did was right, and whenever they saw Manny Abrahams — those that wanted to know how I was going to vote — saw Manny Abrahams vote one way, that settled it.

Q. And he voted for Mr. Lorimer ? — A. Yes, sir.

Q. I suppose you had an understanding with Mr. Abrahams that he was going to vote for Mr. Lorimer ? — A. Oh, yes; with all of them — with all of them.

Q. And that was the criterion ? — A. Well, it was understood before the roll was called at all that morning by them all, those of my crowd.

So, Mr. Browne, the leader of his crowd in the legislature, controlling the vote of Manny Abrahams, who voted as he wished, right or wrong, Mr. Browne, the leader of this crowd, voted for Mr. Lorimer, and the crowd voted, following the bellwether, Manny Abrahams. He procured them to vote as the agent of Lorimer, secured by him to act for him, closeted with him by day and by night, reporting to him step by step, having the relation to him of a member of a campaign committee.

The inquiry narrows down to the question how Mr. Browne secured the adherence of that thirty of the faithful of his crowd who followed the bellwether. How did he secure them? What was his relation to them? It is a broad question which furnishes, when answered, a background against which all the testimony in this case must be considered and weighed.

The air of Springfield at the time was full of suspicion as to the way in which Mr. Browne controlled his crowd, as to the way in which Democratic votes were being secured. A stanch old Democrat, a Mr. Donohue, who was a member of the house and who did not vote for Mr. Lorimer, but stood by his party candidate, testified in explaining some remarks that he may have made, some questions that had been put as to the suspicion that there was bribery, and he said:

That was the general talk, and I could not trace it down; I could not tell now who said it, and then that kind of died away, and then after the election of Mr. Lorimer the thing started again that they were — everything was not straight down there at Springfield with reference to the election of United States Senator. And everybody, I think — I was suspicious myself about the way things went down there. Of course, I didn't have any direct evidence, only from general appearance, I could not see why so many Democrats were going over in a body to vote for a Republican. They may have had reasons, and be more liberal in their views than I am, and might have gone over. I could not see it that way. I am a Democrat, and I am a pretty strong partisan.

Of course suspicions are not evidence, but Mr. Donohue's view, taken at the time of this transaction, is evidence that an honest Democrat who was there saw no party policy or principle which was sufficient to account in his mind for the votes of these fifty-three Democrats for a Republican Senator. If there were motives of patriotism or policy actuating the fifty-three, they were motives locked in their own bosoms and not apparent to the other Democrats who were there.

On the floor of the assembly, on the day of the election before the vote was cast, Mr. English, a member of the house, in effect charged corruption.

Mr. Browne, for the apparent purpose of strengthening his followers, had made a speech in which he had undertaken to explain what was about to be done, and he had used the expression " we cannot cash dreams ", when that stout Democrat of the house retorted, " but you can cash votes ", and it was under the aspersion of that remark in the open house that the votes were cast.

Mr. Groves, a reputable and unimpeached witness, testified that shortly before the election a former member of the legislature came to his room in the hotel, approached him upon the subject of voting for Mr. Lorimer, and said to him: " It might be a good thing for both of us." Groves retorted that " there is not money enough in Springfield to buy my vote for Lorimer "; and he denounced him with such indignation and vehemence that the visitor exclaimed against his talking so loudly with the transom open. Groves exposed that on the floor of the assembly before the election.

Mr. Groves testifies also to a conversation before the election with Mr. Shaw, one of the men who voted for Mr. Lorimer, who was then about to vote for Mr. Lorimer, in which Mr. Groves, his suspicions excited by the attempt made upon him, put the question to Mr. Shaw, how much there was in it to vote for Lorimer. Mr. Groves testifies that Mr. Shaw said there was a thousand dollars in it, as he understood, for the men who would vote for Mr. Lorimer.

Mr. Terrill, an unimpeached and reputable witness, who did not vote for Mr. Lorimer, testifies to this:

A. Well, Mr. Griffin, a member of the house also; I think he comes from Cook County, but I don't remember what district. He never made me any offer of cash. He asked me to vote for Mr. Lorimer. I asked him what there would be in it, and he said, "A thousand dollars, anyway."

Mr. Griffin was one of the faithful thirty that followed the bellwether, and Mr. Terrill told of that approach, of that assault upon his integrity.

Mr. Meyers, another member of the house who did not vote for Mr. Lorimer, testifies that Mr. Browne asked him to vote for Mr. Lorimer. Mr. Browne himself, the agent whose relations to this vote we are inquiring about, asked him to vote for Lorimer:

Q. Will you tell the committee what, if any, conversation you then had with Mr. Browne? — A. I went down to his desk and sat down on a chair right beside him, and he says: "We are going to put this over today, and I would like you to go with us." I says: "Lee, I can't do it."

Q. What else? — A. Then he says that there are some good state jobs to give away and the ready necessary. I says: "I can't help it; I can't go with you."

Q. "The ready necessary," that is correct, is it, that I repeat? — A. Yes, sir.

Mr. Meyers, being interrogated further, said:

Mr. AUSTRIAN. What did you understand that Mr. Browne meant when he said "plenty of the ready necessary"?

The WITNESS. I suppose he meant money; I did not know what else.

So, Mr. President, I say that at the time these votes were cast the air of Springfield was murky with suspicion of corruption, a suspicion now justified by the testimony of these unimpeached, honorable, credible witnesses, of attempt after attempt upon the integrity of the members of the Democratic party in the assembly of Illinois, including this attempt by Lee O'Neil Browne in person.

Mr. Holstlaw, who was a senator, testified that Senator Broderick, a Democratic senator, as was Holstlaw, assured him that there was $2,500 in it for him if he voted for Lorimer, and he did. Holstlaw has also testified to the payment of the $2,500. I shall discuss the testimony regarding that at a later period.

Three other witnesses have testified not merely to approaches, but to the actual payment of money. Mr. White, who was the originator of the charges, Mr. Link, another Democratic member of the assembly, Mr. Beckemeyer, another, all members of the faithful thirty.

Mr. President, it may be that all these men swore falsely. It may be that White, and Link, and Beckemeyer, and Holstlaw, and Meyers, and Groves, and Terrill all perjured themselves. But we are not at liberty to reject their testimony unless it is overcome by countervailing testimony of sufficient weight or unless it is found to be at variance with the true and accepted facts. And the great fact against which all of this evidence is to be considered, that furnishes the background for all these events, is this fact of the relation of Lorimer's agent, Browne, to his followers, and that fact, that underlying fact, which will either corroborate or contradict all these oaths, is established not only by a preponderance of evidence, but beyond that reasonable doubt which is permitted to stand in the way of a verdict that may cost a defendant his liberty or his life.

It happens, Mr. President, that there were two events — two meetings of followers of Browne — subsequent to the election of Lorimer in which the testimony fixes the payment of money, under such circumstances that, if the testimony be believed, there was plain bribery. The first meeting was on the twenty-first of June following the election. The second meeting was on the fifteenth of July. Both meetings were held in St. Louis. At the first the testimony of Beckemeyer and White and Link shows a distribution of a thousand dollars each to the followers of Browne in southern Illinois, and at the second meeting, the fifteenth of July, the testimony of the same men shows a distribution of $900 each to the followers of Browne in southern Illinois.

Mr. Browne has testified that there were three meeting places where his crowd was in the habit of being called together — those of northern Illinois, in Chicago; those of central Illinois, in Springfield; and those of southern Illinois, in St. Louis. At the meeting on the fifteenth of July, when the $900 dividend was made, all the members of Mr. Browne's following in southern Illinois were present, having been summoned to that meeting by telegrams sent to them through Mr. Browne's private secretary or stenographer, Mr. Giblin.

The testimony of Link and Beckemeyer and White to the payment of the $900 to each is disputed. It is disputed only by the testimony of Mr. Wilson, who went to that meeting for Mr. Browne, in Mr. Browne's place. The testimony is corroborated, however, by several very important and indisputable facts. Of course, it is the testimony of three men against one; it is the testimony of three men who say they received the money against one who says he did not pay it. But it appears in the testimony that a year after the meeting was held, and when inquiry came to be made regarding the payment of money to these members of the legislature at that meeting, a false and fictitious and manufactured explanation of the purpose of the meeting was made up. Two of the members who were there testified to Wilson's, who went there as Browne's agent, and, they say, distributed the money, sending them letters in 1910, on the eve of the inquiry, dated back prior to July 15, 1909, and suggesting as a reason for the meeting a proposal to give a banquet to Mr. Browne.